Now I'm Talking

Life Lessons from a
Telecommunications Pioneer

Vijendran Watson

PARTRIDGE

A Penguin Random House Company

To order additional copies of this book, contact
Toll Free 800 101 2657 (Singapore)
Toll Free 1 800 81 7340 (Malaysia)
orders.singapore@partridgepublishing.com

www.partridgepublishing.com/singapore

Contents

For Sharadha, Viruben, Isabelle and Naomi

Preface

It was an unusually cool morning in Yangon. I had flown into Myanmar from Malaysia the previous day and had expected similar humid, hot weather. Instead, there was a slight chill in the air. The country previously known as Burma had been under a military dictatorship. After decades of isolation, Myanmar had slowly begun opening up to the outside world. This had started the previous year.

As I prepared for the meetings in the day ahead, I felt privileged and blessed to be able to witness and experience yet another country use mobile communication as its instrument of change. I had seen it before in Sri Lanka, Bangladesh, and India. I had seen how opening the market to global competition and introducing mobile phones transformed the lives of ordinary people.

Myanmar was the last frontier in Asia for our industry. Yangon, at this time, was crowded with all the known players in the mobile communications industry. They were all looking for a slice of the action. The only two hotels that could be rated with four stars, the Traders Hotel and the Park Royal Hotel, were also making the most of it. They were charging over four times what you would have expected to pay in a similar hotel in Kuala Lumpur. Most of the visitors from the industry were in either one of these two hotels. Everyone knew what the others were doing. Having been involved in the industry since its inception, I could recognise and knew many of the companies present and vying for a slice of the action.

It was 2014. I was working for the Axiata Group of companies based in Kuala Lumpur in Malaysia. Axiata under the leadership of Dato' Sri Jamaludin Bin Ibrahim had grown to be one of the largest telecommunications companies in Asia. They had over 250 million mobile-phone customers on their networks in many countries in Asia.

Edotco was the name of the newest venture, a new infrastructure company that had been set up within the group. It was a start-up that was formed to own and share the infrastructure assets of the group in Malaysia, Sri Lanka, Bangladesh, and Cambodia. I had joined the company the previous year and had moved with my wife to Malaysia.

The lobby area was large in both these hotels. There were multiple meetings going on in every corner. I joined my colleague in one corner of the Traders Hotel with a potential logistics supplier.

Myanmar had already been through the first wave of visitors from our industry. The country opened up by inviting bidding for two potential licenses for mobile communications earlier in the year. Over twelve large, multinational, mobile-phone operators had expressed interest and had their teams in the country.

They in turn employed various consultants, analysts, and bankers from around the world. Representatives from these firms had all been in the country, searching for answers to a plethora of questions before putting in a bid to the government. Since the country was isolated, there was not much data or information available outside. You had to be in the country searching for the information required. In order to put in a bid with the right price for the license, you had to first estimate the cost of building from scratch a whole ecosystem for a new industry in mobile communications.

Finally, after a surprisingly short process, two international companies were chosen—Telenor from Norway and Ooreedo from Qatar. A further two local companies, the incumbent government-owned MPT and another government-linked company, YTP, were also awarded licenses.

I was in the midst of the second wave of visitors into Myanmar. These were the vendors of equipment, of services, logistics suppliers, consultants, infrastructure companies who were now pitching to the successful four licensees to get their share of this action. This was the frenzy I was witnessing. It was reminiscent of a gold rush.

As I sat in the lounge and observed the various meetings, I could envisage the conversations of the seller and the buyer and how, in time as they move to the next meeting, sometimes the seller becomes the buyer. As I observed, I was reminded of my own experience and pioneering efforts working in countries like Sri Lanka, Bangladesh, and India as they first introduced mobile communications and transformed their economies.

I remember the time when it took even the most influential businessman in those countries two years to get a fixed telephone line. Residential applications took even longer. I remember the time when we all thought the mobile phone was a rich man's toy and that this fad would pass away.

Yet within a few years of introducing the mobile phone and competition between providers in these markets, the lives of ordinary people changed.

The fisherman off the coast of Chilaw in Sri Lanka was informing his contacts on shore, via his mobile phone, the details of his catch, and the sales had already been done when the crew returned. The three-wheeler rikshawala at the junction on the streets in Dhaka, Bangladesh, was on the phone arranging his next passenger.

The construction labourer in Mumbai was able to send cash through his mobile phone to his family in remote Bihar, one of the poorest places in India. I had witnessed this amazing transformation in the lives of these ordinary people and how the mobile phone had released entrepreneurial talent and had opened new opportunities for all of them. I was proud that I had played a small part in that change.

Those experiences and thirty-six years of working and living in England, Nigeria, Australia, Sri Lanka, Bangladesh, India, and Malaysia has inspired me to share. Writing a book would be a way to introspect and maybe understand why I made the choices that I did. Writing things down in a book forces you to think and reflect a lot more. It can be a way to understand the motivation, the connection to things spiritual. It could be a cleansing act. It would allow me to get to know myself a little bit more.

My life story in itself is not important. Each one of us is unique, and there is no right or wrong. My hope is that by telling my story and the lessons I learnt, someone will make choices that he or she might have otherwise not have made—a choice that allows him or her to find out the man or woman each of them ought to be.

I was living and working in Kuala Lumpur, Malaysia, seven years ago when I first wrote about the choices we are faced with and how our ancestors made choices that benefitted us, how we in turn have made choices for our children. The book was circulated to just family and close friends. The feedback I received has encouraged me to write again and to make this book more relevant and available to a wider audience. Is it a coincidence that I am back living in Kuala Lumpur as I write this book?

I am not sure, but I accept these and other subtle signals as encouragement to write and share my journey, thoughts, and wisdom.

This book is very different to the one I circulated among friends and family. The seven years has changed me too.

I am now entering what I call the golden age, starting the seventh decade of my life.

The first twenty years I would categorise as the formative years, the years when I was absorbing and learning, the time of observation and the time when my parents and family and close friends had the greatest influence on me.

Most of the choices in the early years were made for me.

As I grew older, I had a few more choices to make on my own. Most of the more significant choices that I made in the formative years I made with the guidance and after consultation with my parents or elders in the family.

The years from twenty to thirty were the foundation years, the time when I got married, the time when we started a family, the time I built my credentials in my chosen field, the time when I took on risks. These were the years that I started making all choices myself when I was single and with my wife after I got married. Some of the choices worked out and some did not.

The years from thirty to sixty I would categorise as the significant years.

During this time, I was lucky enough to be riding a wave—a wave of the greatest economic growth we have known. I was also blessed to be in an industry that had even more amazing growth in that period. This was the time when our children grew up to be adults, a period where they started their own married lives. Many of the choices made during this time were strongly influenced by the family unit. Many of the choices we made leaving one country for the next were influenced by the needs of the children and their education, the need for stability, the need to give them the best start in life.

I am looking forward to living the golden years, a time when we still have the health and energy to do things we want to do, the time where we have more freedom to do what we enjoy, the time when I am less beholden to keeping a job for the sake of earning a wage. The children have both married and left the nest. My wife Sharadha and I are free to pursue the spiritual growth and travel experiences we both enjoy. It's a good time to publish this book at the dawn of this age.

As I reflect on my life, there have been highs and lows, periods of extreme stress and periods of absolute joy, and yet overall I am blessed to have this sense of satisfaction and contentment. This sense comes primarily from being comfortable with oneself, accepting things as they are.

"The moment will arrive when you are comfortable with who you are, and what you are– bald or old or fat or poor, successful or struggling- when you don't feel the need to apologize for anything or to deny anything. To be comfortable in your own skin is the beginning of strength." – Charles B. Handy.

It comes after years of working at a relationship with your life partner, someone you have let in the closest to your soul and with whom you have found a peaceful compromise.

It comes as we observe our children, who now as young adults are making their own choices in their foundation years. They are both transitioning to the significant years.

This sense also comes when I meet members of a team I had led in the past, young graduates I had employed in their first jobs who are now at the top of their profession, and they recall their own journey and how my leadership and guidance had touched and improved their lives. This feedback is always special.

I recently had a pleasant surprise when an ex-colleague from Lanka Bell got in touch through the business social-networking site called LinkedIn. He is now a successful senior executive in the call centre business. He is based in Canada but travels extensively through the United States and the region.

This is what he wrote:

> You took the risk of handing over the call centre, which was one of the critical functions of the business, to a [twenty-one-year-old], fresh graduate.
>
> The trust you put in my ability made me work twice as hard not only to achieve but exceed your expectations. This is something I continue to believe in even today: Treat people as if they were what they ought to be and you help them to become what they are capable of being.
>
> The decision you took [fourteen] years ago changed my career forever and probably through me changed [a] few other careers.

As I reflect on my journey, there were risks and choices made that enabled me to climb to the top of the ladder in the corporate world. There were many, who supported me along the way and entrusted me with leadership of large teams and million dollar projects. I am extremely grateful to them. Not by desire or choice but I became a dab hand at successfully doing start-up ventures. I had made a successful transition from the little pond of underdeveloped Ceylon, where I grew up as a child and teenager, to the greater ocean of the developed Western world and had not just survived but had risen to the top ranks of management.

As a family unit, we did have our ups and downs, challenges, and moments of joy. We had all the basics we needed in our lives and some modest trappings one would associate with success. Importantly, I felt that the choices Sharadha and I made in our lives, the risks we had taken, had allowed us to be able to give a platform for the children to make a better life for themselves. We are proud of how our children have become the adults they are.

I recognise that it was the choices made by my parents, grandparents and ancestors that gave me the platform, the start, the environment, the circumstances to make my own choices when I reached adulthood. The choices that I made subsequently on my own and those made with Sharadha once I was married allowed us to get here to our home in Sydney, Australia, from the UK.

I had dabbled in writing earlier and had enjoyed it. I had written many articles that were published in the *Lanka Monthly Digest (LMD)*, a business magazine in Sri Lanka. They say there is always one book in every writer, and this is that book.

The nature of the narrative in this book and my preferred style requires that I write in the first person. Yet my life has not been only about "me, myself, and I." Without the support of people around me, without their affection and warmth, without their encouragement, I would not have lasted this journey.

So while my narrative requires me to use a lot of *I*, you must discount its character. You should focus on the journey and the lessons. I have deliberately left out "the wind beneath my wings," Sharadha, and her contribution to my life; her contribution in nurturing and being the rock of our family unit and in dedicating her full time to our children; her contribution to my career success.

I have left these contributions from this book. I was an uncut gem, a raw young person of twenty-seven, when I married Sharadha and we started our relationship and family. Together, we made it happen. I am unworthy to properly describe her contribution to my life in words, and so I won't try. To honour her wishes, I have kept our personal relationship outside the purview of this book.

People who know me have labelled me a quiet person, one who does not say much. I am better at the written word than the spoken. So here is my story. Now I'm talking.

Chapter 1

Start with the End in Mind

It was midday in the centre of the city. We were in a paved public square in Sydney. I was blindfolded. It was the year 1992. I was working for a company called OTC International in Australia. OTC was a government-owned company. It had the monopoly and was solely responsible for all international telecommunications in and out of the country. OTC International was specifically set up by OTC to look for new opportunities outside of Australia.

OTC and Telecom Australia were merged by the government in February that year. The new company was called AOTC. It would later be rebranded to become Telstra.

Together with a number of my colleagues, who were also blindfolded, we were in a line, one hand on the other's shoulder. We were taking instructions from a leader as to how we should reach our destination. Leigh Farnell was standing at that destination. He was standing a short distance away. Only the leader of our group was without a blindfold. He was shouting instructions. The task was made harder as we had to navigate through the crowds of working people pouring out of the office buildings. They were coming out for the sunshine and to have lunch. Left! No! No! Stop! Right...the instructions kept coming from the leader. We were an amusing sight to the crowds.

The communication from the leader was not enough. The team had to keep checking back to ensure the instructions were correct. We learnt some important lessons that day.

Leigh was conducting a corporate training programme on team-building. Through this activity, he was attempting to demonstrate the importance of communication when working in teams. After a morning session in the training room, we were taken out into the fresh air to participate in this and other activities and games to learn by action. This was my introduction to Leigh Farnell.

Leigh was unique in his style and delivery. He could have had a career as a stand-up comic. Instead, he chose to study the behaviour of people and use his comedy to become an excellent facilitator. He knew when to turn up the heat to get people to open up to the core issues or get to the root cause of a problem. He knew how to lighten the mood in the room with some humour and how to cool things down when things got heated and intense.

As I got to know Leigh over time, I invited him to work with me facilitating workshops or when we had an "off-site" team meeting in Sri Lanka, Bangladesh, and Australia. I turned to him whenever I needed that great skill he had of turning a room full of individuals into a team. Leigh also became my coach, mentor, and friend.

Leigh Farnell had grown up in Bendigo, Victoria. He completed a degree in human performance at Melbourne University before earning his masters in physical education in Western Australia. After his masters, he settled in Perth. The connection that Leigh made between sport, leadership, and management was ahead of its time. We now have the likes of Alex Ferguson, the long-time manager of the Manchester United football team, writing on leadership and management, but in the '90s this connection was unique.

I first came across this expression "start with the end in mind" from Leigh. It's a simple concept, a cliché, a well-used management expression, but it is powerful. I have used the concept extensively in my career. Whenever Leigh started a team-building session or workshop, he would always ask the participants what their own expectations were for the workshop and what they were expecting to get out of it. Start with the end in mind.

There is a big difference between a facilitator or trainer who actually practices what he is talking about and one who doesn't. Leigh practised what he preached. There is a big difference between managers and leaders who verbalises various management theories or talks about change in culture and values and then practices it and those who don't. Those leaders I worked for and admired all had this quality, this ability to "walk the talk".

I organised many team-building sessions with Leigh in the many leadership roles I had through Australia and Asia.

Prior to the day of the workshop, Leigh would have spent time with me as the leader and organiser to understand my expectations of the workshop and outcomes that I was expecting. No one can predict how the actual sessions turn out. The objective is to ask the teams to brainstorm new ideas or solutions to problems we are having at work. No one can predict the way the animosity between departments and underlying personal issues are brought out during the sessions. People get defensive. People get territorial. I have observed that people are the same; these reactions are common in the UK and Australia as they are in Sri Lanka, Malaysia, the Philippines, Bangladesh, or India.

We have had many workshops that got quite heated. This was a good sign. It meant the participants were engaged and generating a lot of energy. Issues that had been kept under the surface at work were being discussed and argued. Having the end in mind allowed Leigh, as facilitator, to use this energy. He conducted the sessions in such a way that both the teams and my objectives were met. The sessions were honest and open, and many of my own shortcomings as a leader were highlighted by the team, in addition to the other issues and challenges the team had in working with each other.

We set up an action plan to solve these issues and for me to agree to change my way of working with the team. The team also agreed on how they would change behaviour with each other. The participants always felt a sense of achievement and involvement as they were consulted. Leigh had bothered to ask them what they wanted out of the day before we started and had checked at the end of the day to see if this was achieved. This was unique at that time. I realised the power of starting with the end in mind and consciously used it when starting meetings and embarking on new projects. It did not come naturally, but over time, as I experienced the benefits, it became a habit.

It's 6:00 a.m. in Kuala Lumpur. It's dark. Dawn breaks only around 7:00 a.m. in the valley city. Sharadha and I are living in an apartment, walking distance from my workplace, and close to KL Sentral railway hub. I walk out from the apartment block, around the periphery of KL Sentral station, through the Hilton hotel car park, cross a road, and head towards Lake Park, the botanical gardens in Kuala Lumpur. I am there in less than fifteen minutes. The park is dark, but the pathways around the lake are lit by street lights. It's quiet. I join the few early morning walkers and joggers in the park.

I never set out to make this morning exercise a routine. It has, though, over the years become an essential part of my day wherever I am. I have my favourite route at home in Sydney. A three-kilometre walk up some steep hills around the leafy suburb of Beecroft. I have my favourite walk along the water at the Marina Bay near Nichole

Highway MRT station in Singapore and the Galle Face promenade by the Indian Ocean in Colombo in Sri Lanka. Even in Kolkata, I managed to find a wide street at the back of our apartment in Alipoor. The quiet time has been very therapeutic and has allowed me to work out the solution or the actions that I need to take during the day. It has become addictive.

As I walk around the lake, my mind is full of thoughts. My thoughts are random, from the previous day at work to the issues closer to home with the children, the unresolved challenges. The sky is gradually and softly lighting up with a warm glow of sunrise. It's dawn. The sounds of birds, a few chirps at first, builds to a chorus; the squirrels dart up and down the trees and in and out of the bushes. This quiet time alone, walking, gives me the opportunity to think. I inevitably also think of the day ahead. This quiet time gives me the opportunity to start the day with the end in mind.

Having a plan for the day without being overly ambitious allows you a sense of satisfaction and a sense of achievement at the end of that day. However small your "to-do list" is, having one and ticking it off as you complete the tasks gives you that sense of satisfaction. Not having any plan means you have a sense of unease when you go to bed. This unease creates doubt in your mind, a doubt that multiplies as you think of the tasks still left to be done. When the thoughts of the tasks still left to be done dominate your thinking, you get a sense of not being on top.

I hate this feeling of not being on top of things. I hate this feeling of being overwhelmed by the things still left to do. This prompts me to getting back to listing the things that have been done and to regaining that sense of satisfaction, to celebrate the small achievements of the day rather than be despondent of the tasks yet left unfinished. We have a choice in how we choose to view the day as half empty or as half full.

Writing a book about my life, should I also start with the end in mind?

The end would be death.

Death is the end for our bodies in this life and this journey. I do, however, believe that the journey does continue. The soul moves on.

I don't dwell on the subject, and surprisingly I am not scared of death. However, I have thought about it during quiet moments, come to my own views.

I have accepted that we have no choice in the timing of the end. We have no choice in the manner or circumstances in which we will end this journey and begin the next. It may come in the stealth of the night while we are peacefully asleep. It may come unexpectedly while crossing a road or driving a car. It can be around us like gathering clouds. We know it will rain soon but don't know exactly when, as do most people with a terminal illness such as cancer that has spread widely in the body or those with other terminal illnesses.

I am aware that the end could come right now, at this time in my life, when I am enjoying the fruits of labour, of the last twenty years. It could come as a sudden heart attack, as it did to Dr. Kidman, the father of Australian actress and Hollywood star, Nicole. He was a fit man, lean, as a doctor aware of his diet and lifestyle, and yet on a visit to see his other daughter, Antonia, in Singapore, he suddenly collapsed and died.

I travel and fly continuously on work. It could come on a flight, as it did to the innocent people flying Malaysian Airlines MH17 from Amsterdam to Kuala Lumpur. Or the end will come at the time the body decided it has got to its "use-by date."

I try, as most of us do, not to dwell on the end. I try to focus on what I have control of rather than the things I don't control.

I recall a saying. "It's not the end of the journey that matters; it's the journey that matters in the end."

While we don't have a choice in the nature and the timing of our bodies' ends, we do have a choice on how we approach this inevitable event.

We do have a choice.

Some of us become so obsessed with the end and of dying that we forget to enjoy the journey.

Should we live in constant fear of death or of a disability in old age that we take preventative measures to an extreme? Or should we just leave the fate of whatever and whenever to God and focus on the things we have some control over?

Advances in medicine and research has given us more insights into how the human body functions—how cancer cells are formed and grow, how arteries are blocked and constrict blood and oxygen to the vital organs leading to a heart failure or stroke. We have a lot of information on general health and how the average body functions. I believe that we ignore the fact that each one of us is unique, and all this knowledge may not be relevant. I believe we ignore the subtle messages coming from our bodies.

Many of us, including myself, are persuaded mainly by the medical profession and health experts that we have some control somehow, that we are in control of having a longer life, of cheating death, of not suffering in later life with a stroke or diabetes or senile dementia. They recommend that we stuff ourselves with medication, vitamins, certain fruits, certain nuts, and certain herbs and take endless tests— blood tests, urine tests.

The knowledge gained from these tests further persuades us to take it to experts, who interpret the results based on their experience to recommend further medication or surgery. In retrospect, many times the expert's advice was the correct interpretation of the results.

Many more times the interpretation was wrong.

This leads you into a circle of being in and out of the doctors or hospital and being on expensive medication. Obsessed with the knowledge of these tests and the information on the Internet, we fail to live the opportunity of the day—a day that disappears forever when we go to bed.

I am as guilty too, in this flawed thought process. We are pressured by family and doctors to think this way.

We focus on preventing death.

We focus on preventing death, which we know will definitely come in its good time. We forget to live life, to enjoy the day, to enjoy the food and wine, to say "g'day" to a stranger, to help our neighbours and those in need, to say "I love you" to those close to us who we sometimes take for granted.

I met Charles Handy in New Delhi, India, in 2007. Charles is in his eighties, a full head of white hair, a quintessential Englishman. He is the pioneer in introducing the MBA programs in the UK, and a person who has been sharing his wisdom for many years. He is an author of thought-provoking management books, some of which I have read and enjoyed. I had the pleasure of meeting him at the sidelines of a conference on the "Future of Work." I was living and working in Gurgaon close to Delhi in India. Nokia, who I was working for at the time, had organised a private session for senior managers with him.

In his book, *Myself and Other Important Matters*, he contends that life is really a search for our own identity. "Sad," Charles says, "is he or she who dies without really knowing who they really are, or of what they are really capable."

I agree with Charles, but I go further to say that in addition, we all have a purpose in life. Our life should be about finding that purpose. If we don't find that purpose early in our lives, maybe we will find it later. Some of us are late bloomers. In the search of that purpose, we find out more about ourselves and our identity.

Some of us will eventually find that purpose; others will keep searching and may not succeed. That's OK. But it's important to keep searching.

Searching for that purpose means making choices that have risks, opening doors without knowing what's beyond, wrenching ourselves from our comfort zone.

There is no need to plan for the end, I just need to be mindful that daily, I need to be making a difference to someone and discovering something more about myself.

Starting with the end in mind, that's how I like to view the end—a constant search for my identity and purpose.

"The two most important days in your life are the day you are born and the day you find out why"- Mark Twain.

My life started in London, around 11:00 a.m. on the nineteenth of March in 1955.

London in the '50s was much like Beijing is today, full of soot and pollution. London was famous for its foggy days, the bus conductor walking in front of the bus to guide the driver as he could not see the road for the fog. This was a time in Britain when there were very few Asians. It was a mainly white England.

I was born at the Middlesex Hospital in London, a rare sight for the nursing staff. Here I was, dark skinned with a full head of black hair, no chance of a mix up with another baby. I was part novelty. Just before I was born my mother caught the chicken pox. At that time, this was a highly contagious and relatively unknown disease. Immediately after my birth, both my mother and I were taken to another hospital and put in isolation. I was born with chicken pox.

As a newborn, I could not be kept with other babies in the ward. I later learnt that babies who catch chicken pox so early in life nearly always end up with brain damage. How I did not have any lasting effects of that disease can only be described as God's grace. My mother recently told me that had she known about the long-lasting effects of chicken pox then, she would have been pulling her hair out with concern. Luckily, she was blissfully ignorant about the consequences at that time.

On that same day, a few hundred kilometres away in Baumbholder, Idar-Oberstein, in Germany, Bruce Willis, the Hollywood actor, was also born. In that year of 1955, several million babies were born all over the world. We were still in the era called the "baby boom." Those born in 1955 included Kevin Costner, Indira Nooyi, Nandan Nilekani, John Grisham, Rowan Atkinson, Greg Schmidt, Greg Norman, Ian Botham, Jerry Seinfeld, Steve Jobs, and Bill Gates just to name a few—all newborn babies; all equal in the eyes of God; the apple of their parents' eyes and of no significance to anyone else at the time of birth; and all with a journey to discover their purposes in life.

Sir Winston Churchill was the prime minister in England at the time, but not for long as he had to resign within weeks in early April that year. The British Empire was in decline; it was coming to its end. Most of the far eastern counties were already independent.

How did I come to be born in London?

It was 1935. Vernon was eight years old. He had just moved to live at their home on Beach Road in Mount Lavinia. Mount Lavinia was a hamlet on the coast, a few miles south of the capital Colombo, in Ceylon. Ceylon was under British rule, part of the Empire.

Mount Lavinia was the favourite holiday spot of the British governors during their rule of Ceylon. The current Mount Lavinia Hotel was previously the governor's residence and was built in 1806. Governor Thomas Maitland built the residence, and during his visits there fell in love with the dancer Lovinia Aponsuwa. She was half Portuguese and half Sinhalese and was a dancer in her father's troupe. The governor fell passionately in love with Lovinia and constructed an underground tunnel so he could meet her secretly. As a token of his affection, he named the governor's mansion "Mount Lavinia." The surrounding area then took the name from the mansion.

In 1935, Mount Lavinia was still the place one went to for holidays to enjoy the sea air and beach. The roads were narrow and only few owned cars. Most of the traffic was horse and carriage or bullock carts. Colombo to Mount Lavinia was a long ride. Vernon was one of seven boys, children of Gunam and Emily. Gunam was diagnosed with an incurable condition, a cyst in his kidney, three years earlier in 1932. He was in pain and bedridden and needed constant care. He and Emily and the seven boys had decided to move to Mount Lavinia where they owned a house by the sea. It was felt the sea air would ease his suffering. Mount Lavinia also had a prominent Anglican School called St. Thomas' College where the boys could be educated. For three years, Emily cared and made the pain bearable for Gunam. In 1935, Gunam passed away.

The eldest of the seven boys, Hector was eighteen, and the youngest, Dalton, was five. Emily, who had mentally prepared herself for this outcome, moved back to Bambalapitiya, a suburb of Colombo. She moved back with her sons to the house her husband, Gunam, had built called "Gunagiri."

After the death of her husband, Emily had a choice.

She had a choice to depend on her extended family for support or to take ownership of her situation and be independent. Emily chose the latter. In a period in history when women were very much in the home, seen and not heard, Emily made a bold choice to manage by herself, be a single parent and to educate her seven boys.

Emily was fortunate. She had been left some properties both by her father and by Gunam, who was a successful solicitor. Emily rented these properties and used the proceeds to build many more houses in the suburbs of Mount Lavinia, Bambalapitiya, and Cinnamon Gardens. She supervised the construction and maintained the properties and used the rent to educate her seven boys. Emily made a choice with huge risks, but the returns were that all her boys went on to be professionals in the independent Ceylon. On his deathbed, it was the wish of Gunam that the two younger boys, Vernon and Dalton, should have some money put aside and be sent to England to complete their studies.

Vernon was a bright student and very focused on his studies. He wasn't into sports and other distractions at St. Thomas' College. After completing school, he entered university, and he completed his bachelor's degree in science at the University of Colombo in 1948, the year of independence of Ceylon from years of colonial rule.

Irene was born in Colombo. Her father, Vijayam, a surgeon, was posted in Badulla at that time. Badulla was a quaint town in the hills, located in the centre of Ceylon, a town surrounded by lush tea estates managed by the British colonial tea companies at that time. Irene was born in the house of her maternal grandfather, Lawton, in Colombo. It was a home birth and one supervised by her father. Irene and her elder sister, Christine, grew up in the various locations their father was posted to and grew with a self-confidence that only comes with this constant displacement early in one's life. It helped them adapt to change.

In 1948, the year of independence for Ceylon, Vernon already had his degree. He could have joined the public service as an engineer or remained as a lecturer in the university, something he wanted to do. However, this legacy wish by his father to complete his education in England was available, and Emily was keen that he pursue his studies in England. This was easier said than done. While there were no visa or emigration formalities, as Ceylon was part of the British Empire, the cost to go by ship and support oneself in England was huge. Emily had to sell off one of the properties to fulfil the wish of her late husband. Vernon was naturally very attached to his mother since, as a single parent, she had nurtured him to adulthood. It was a difficult choice, one made not knowing the outcome or the risks. The war in Europe had ended in 1945; three years later England was still recovering, many of its cities bombed and in ruins. Life in Ceylon was relatively more stable. It was a difficult choice that Vernon made. A choice that was to take him on journey of a career in telecommunications, to reach the pinnacle of that career by being the chairman of Sri Lanka Telecom, and steering that organisation from being a government department to a corporation.

Vernon left for England in July 1948 with a British passport. Ceylon, independent since February that year, had not yet got its own passport designed and printed. It was probably lower on the country's list of priorities as the number of citizens travelling would have been very few. Vernon completed his second degree in electrical engineering, this time specialising in a new branch of engineering called telecommunications, and returned to Ceylon, again with an intention of joining the university as a lecturer. He contacted Prof. Paul for an opening in the electrical engineering faculty and was told that the position had been already filled. The Ceylon post office, in the meantime, was looking for fresh engineers. Vernon applied and was taken in as an engineer.

Vernon had known Irene, who was five years younger than him, most of his life. Vernon's father Gunam and Irene's father Vijayam were first cousins and had at one time lived in the same house while growing up. Vijayam and Gunam were very close. Vijayam went on to become a surgeon and Gunam a lawyer. Even after their respective marriages to Louisa and Emily, Vijayam and Gunam remained great friends. As a young surgeon, Vijayam was posted to various parts of Ceylon while Gunam practised law in Colombo. Whenever Vijayam came down to Colombo from his outstation posting, either for a weekend or for a function, he would immediately, after getting home and unpacking, visit his friend Gunam and usually take the family with him. After Gunam died, Vijayam, who was fond of the young Vernon, would invite him during the school holidays to Galle. Vijayam was working in Galle at that time. Since Galle was not too far from Colombo, Vernon would travel with one of his brothers to spend a few days with Vijayam and his family. It was how Vernon and Irene got to know each other from a very early age.

In 1954, on February 8, Vernon married Irene and immediately after the wedding, set sail for England. Prior to the wedding, Vernon had been selected with a few other engineers and awarded a scholarship by the British Post Office to learn more about the practical aspects of running a telecommunication network.

When Vernon and Irene found out they were going to have a child, they had a choice. They either let Irene stay in London and have the child or return to Ceylon where they would be under the care of

Irene's father who was a doctor and have the support of the extended family. This would be Vijayam and Louisa's first grandchild. Vernon's brother Donald also a doctor was in London at that time. He advised Vernon to send Irene home to Ceylon to have this first baby. His view was that the expenses involved in bringing up a baby in London would be high and on his meagre scholarship allowance Vernon might find it hard to cope. Vijayam advised them to have the baby in London and to manage the expenses. They chose to stay and take the risk.

This was how I came to be born in London, to Vernon my father and Irene, my mother.

My parents made their choice based on economic and practical considerations. Would they be able to support having a baby in London? They were strangers and visitors in this land. They knew the alternative of sending my mum back to Ceylon was a safe bet. There she would be taken care of by her doctor father and the extended family, a large house with all its comforts. A home with live-in hired help. It would also have absolved them of some of the responsibility that goes with having a first child. Many parents would have taken that option. When the child was born with Chicken Pox and in danger of its life they might have wondered if they had indeed made the right choice. The choice they made was to struggle in a small room in Kensington, to take the risk, to manage with the scholarship allowance they were given.

My mother was innovative. She converted one of her suitcases into the cot. She stitched and lined the suitcase to make it comfortable. The government helped with milk and other essentials. Medical services were free. She had friends who helped. She kept many coins to feed the meter that kept the heating on. The only heater in the room was kept close to the cot. On a cold March day with snow outside, I was welcomed to their small room at 45, Scarsdale Villas, Kensington, in London.

That risk was rewarded richly in 1974, nineteen years after I was born. I had to leave Sri Lanka in a hurry to take up a place at the University of Salford. After a very ordinary advanced level results, my chances were slim, and I had given up hope of going to study in the UK. Suddenly, however a place had become available. I had to join immediately. The country of Sri Lanka was ruined by student unrest, food rationing, and an inept socialist government. The Government had placed restrictions on travel abroad. Everyone needed an exit visa. You could not take more than a few sterling pounds out of the country. England had become stricter with its immigration, and there was still a process and a period of waiting to get the student visa. My British birth gave me an automatic right to a passport. I applied and got that in a few days and left for England.

Six months after my birth my mother decided to take me back to Ceylon. It was a long journey by sea, just my mother and me. We travelled on the MS *Oranje*, a Dutch ship. A postcard sent by my mother to her mother from the port of Aden reads as follows:

"We have had very fine weather and a very pleasant journey so far. Baby is feeling the heat a bit. There is an outbreak of measles on board. The boat is expected there on the fifteenth morning. Love to all at house from baby and self. Irene."

I arrived in Ceylon, this island paradise, where I lived for the next nineteen years.

Chapter 2

Growing Up in Paradise

When we are born, it's ground zero. We are pure, with no preconceptions. We have no religious beliefs and no sense of values. All of these get shaped and influenced at an early age by our parents, the school we attend, the friends we keep, the environment, and family.

If I had grown up in London, I would have been a different person. I would have had the same parents, but they would have behaved differently in the different environment. My life would have been completely different. I believe that I was influenced early in life by my parents, the schools I attended, the friends I grew up with, my grandparents and certain elders in the extended and close knit family who influenced me more than others.

The MS Oranje docked in the port of Colombo.

There to greet their daughter Irene and her six-month-old baby was her welcoming family. The journey had taken many days. The only communication with their daughter the past year had been through letters. In this age of e-mail, it is hard to imagine that a reply to a letter could take up to a month or more. At that time letters also travelled by sea.

I was their first grandchild, the eldest grandson. The first to carry me was my grandmother Louisa. My grandfather Vijayam was there and his brother Devanayagam, all three on my mother's side of the family, who were to have a significant influence in my life.

Ceylon was still finding its way in 1955. The country was just seven years into independence. The coronation of Queen Elizabeth II had taken place in 1952. The queen had made her first visit to Ceylon the previous year and took back with her, the last British governor-general, Viscount Soulbury. The first local governor-general Sir Oliver Goonetileka, was her new representative. Sir John Kotelawala was the prime minister of the island nation. In the seven years since independence, he was already the third prime minister.

The Island was simmering with political tensions beneath the surface. The British, left behind a good education system, their values, English as a uniting language, democracy and the rule of law. They tried in the last years of their reign but had not solved the minority or majority community concerns.

These divisions between the communities, they had deliberately fuelled in order to rule the country with as little resources as possible. They had ruled the island for 133 years, and it had produced their needs of tea, rubber, and spices. It was an essential stopping point on their journey to the rest of their colonies in the far east of Asia. They had enjoyed the Island and its strategic location. Leaving the Island was hard.

The British had granted Independence in 1948, yet seven years later, they still had control and authority over the strategic natural harbour and naval base at Trincomalee located on the north east of the Island. They also had authority and control over the air force base at Katunayake near Colombo. The ugly side of their colonial legacy still remained. The Colombo Swimming Club, for example, a private, members-only club, was still for whites only.

From the port of Colombo, I was taken to the most wonderful large house that I would call home for the next nineteen years.

Colombo was a comparatively well-developed city for Asia at that time. There were trams running in the centre of the city. A bustling commercial hub had developed around the harbour. Many ships travelling to between England and Australia would stop in Colombo for a rest. The passengers keen to stretch their legs would walk around the city. There were department stores such as Cargill's and Millers for shopping, souvenir sellers, entertainment by the snake charmers, elephant rides, rickshaw pullers stood by with their rickshaws looking for passengers to take to their destinations. This form of transport was the accepted norm. The suburbs of Colombo only stretched for a few miles east of the harbour. The rest was open fields of paddy, dense thicket, and jungle.

I was arriving in Colombo to be part of a unique generation. A generation that grew up as children in an Independent Ceylon. We had reached the age of seventeen and were close to becoming adults when Ceylon unshackled itself from the Queen as head of state and became the Republic of Sri Lanka. My parents were part of the last generation educated under colonial rule. They spoke only English at home. I spoke only English from the time I could speak. I thought in English. English became my mother tongue.

From the city of Colombo crossing the wide open green that is known as Galle Face, if you travel along the Galle road you will arrive at the suburb of Colpetty. Now known as Kollupitiya. In 1955, Colpetty was one of many, then-fully residential, quiet suburbs of Colombo. Apart from a few commercial premises on the Galle Road the rest of the suburb was residential. The home, was two conjoined houses that looked like one large building. The two houses had ten bedrooms and a front that straddled two streets.

One of the houses was divided into two separate apartments, one up and one down. My grandparents, my two grand-uncles, with my mother's two younger siblings lived in one house. Our family and my mother's elder sister's family stayed in the two apartments of the other house. I was in and out of all of the three homes, and they were one to me.

My father returned later that year having finished his training with the British post office. He was appointed as an assistant engineer in the Ceylon post office with a salary of Rs 500 a month. The rupee then was Rs 13.33 to the British pound.

Today, I reflect with gratitude the blessing of the protective, nurturing environment these conjoined houses with this large, extended family gave to me as a child growing up—running from my parent's apartment on the top floor of one house when I was bored to the next house, where my grandparents lived, or to the downstairs apartment, where my aunt Christine lived, all without leaving the boundary of this great house.

Running in and out from one house to the other, there was no shortage of people to interact with—from my mother's elder sister, Christine, and her husband, Chandi; to my grandmother and Missiya, my grandmother's domestic help, who was a part of the family; a cousin, Surendran, six months younger to me who was a brother and an accomplice in the mischief we got up to; a sister, Shalini, who came two years after me and completed the trio of young children growing up in this large house. In addition, there were my mother's two younger siblings, my uncle Vijayakumar who was seven years older than me and a slightly older aunt, Kamala. And finally there were the two bachelors, my grandfather's brothers,

Devanayagam and Babba. As a baby, my grand-uncle Devanayagam would spend hours just carrying me and walking around. As I grew older, he would take me out in his old car whenever he was visiting his many friends.

For a young boy, there was so much to absorb. There was a swing in the garden. There was the shaggy pet dog, Rusty. There was so much love and no shortage of people to spoil and shower you with love.

Since we lived with my mother's family, I got closer to them.

My grandfather Vijayam was a surgeon working at Rutnam's, a private hospital. I remember the respect and panic he generated whenever he was around. The house clearly worked around him. He was dark and tall. He had this demeanour of authority and a deep voice. A voice gravelled by the fifty cigarettes he smoked in a day. He was a kind man, who always had a sweet in his pocket for his "*sithamany*" as he used to call me.

My grandmother Louisa was very special too. She was fair in complexion, much shorter than my grandfather, she was gentle yet you always sensed a strong person behind her persona. She ran the house making it look simple and no bother. As I look back, I often wonder at the work that must have gone into feeding all of us in the large house. There was always a snack or tea available for the many visitors who came to see my grandfather. Most visitors turned up unannounced.

The neighbourhood was so quiet. The streets were safe and free of traffic. There were many boys and girls of our age who lived down the street. As we grew up, we explored beyond the gates of our house and formed great friendships with the neighbours. We played cricket on the street. It was a wonderful era. It was an era when the whole island of Ceylon, now called Sri Lanka, had a population of only 8 million people.

Christmas was always special. Every year a few weeks before Christmas, there was the annual family party hosted by my grandparents. My grandfather was the eldest male among many brothers and sisters in a very large family. We would have forty and fifty guests, just in the extended family, uncles, aunts and cousins. The excitement of the party, for me, started with shopping for all the gifts with my grandmother; the wrapping of the gifts with my mother, my sister Shalini, and cousin Surendran and aunts; the making of the fruity Christmas cake. The Santa for the party was always a mystery. It was one of my mother's cousins, Ronald or Carlyle, but dressed so well in costume it was difficult to guess.

New Year's Eve celebrations are part of the relished childhood memories. The adults in this family would go for the watch night service at the local Methodist church, a church service that straddled the transition of the old and new year, from about 11:00 p.m. to some minutes past midnight. We three, Surendran, Shalini, and I, would be sleeping under the watchful eye of Missiya. Close to midnight we would be woken up by the loud noise of the firecrackers heralding in the New Year and aroma of strong coffee brewing. A little later the full extended family would drop in after the service for a cup of coffee and cake. These were special times, an annual family tradition now lost forever as the extended family is spread to all parts of the globe.

The area of the suburb of Colpetty where we have our family home was once a swampy low lying bushy area that was originally at some point of time on the shores of the Beira Lake. Over a period of time the Beira Lake shrunk and the land was drained and reclaimed. We constantly had floods when there was a heavy shower during the monsoon. Colombo was a small city in the 1920s, and the more popular residential areas of that time were close to the fort and Pettah, the commercial centres.

It was my great-grandfather Alfred Lawton who persuaded his son-in-law, my grandfather Vijayam, to buy land in this reclaimed, new area of Colombo. It's hard to imagine now, but the area was an overgrown jungle of close knit banana plants and small dirt tracks for bullock carts. It would certainly have been a challenge to build these two conjoined houses.

Alfred Lawton was the father of my Grandmother Louisa. He was a businessman who made his money in Insurance. He had a good knack for looking at an ugly moth and spotting the beautiful butterfly. Knowing my grandfather was too busy pursuing his career as a surgeon in the outstations of Ceylon, he volunteered to supervise the construction of these two houses in Colombo. Every day he would come from his home with a packed lunch and supervise the building of this house.

Our privileged situation in life then and today, owes a lot to many of our ancestors who worked hard at the opportunity they were given and left a legacy for the next generation to build on. Two of the grandfathers on my mother's side, stand out in that respect. Alfred Lawton and Timothy Nevins Selvadurai.

Alfred Lawton was comfortable in an affluent Ceylon in the early 1900s. Ceylon then was thriving on a very vibrant tea industry. Alfred made a choice. A choice with considerable risks. He chose to leave the relative stability and comfort of Ceylon and seek opportunity in a new and developing territory of Malaya in east of the British Empire. Malaya was going through a boom in Tin and Rubber. The British needed educated men with some experience to develop this part of the Empire and help to extract its wealth.

Many Ceylonese were recruited by the British in Ceylon and taken to help administer British Malaya. The Tamils from the north of Ceylon, in particular were preferred, because of their education, a legacy of American Christian missionaries. Alfred applied for a job in the Insurance field and was accepted.

He left with his newlywed wife, Thangamma, and went to work in Kuala Lumpur. The choice paid off. He was successful in his field of insurance and had a comfortable life in Kuala Lumpur. He and his wife were blessed with three daughters, all born in Malaya—my grandmother, Louisa, and her two sisters, Mary and Leena. The story changed when, sadly, Alfred's wife, Thangamma, died during a holiday in Ceylon.

Alfred decided to sell up and return. When he returned to Ceylon, Alfred Lawton invested the money he had made in Malaya, in property. He was able to give each of his three daughters a handsome dowry and marry them well according to the customs of that time.

My great-grandfather, Timothy Nevins Selvadurai, was a dedicated teacher, a high achiever, in the field of education. Education was not universal in Ceylon. He was recognised and awarded the British Empire Medal for Meritorious Service in the 1923 Birthday Honours of King George V. This was awarded for his services to education.

He took to politics later in his life and was elected as a Member of The State Legislature in the Colonial Ceylon parliament, elected as the representative for seat of Kayts in the North of Ceylon in 1934. In the legislature, he was known as the "Silver-Tongued Orator" for his eloquent speeches. He was a contributor to the reform of the constitution of Ceylon.

Timothy's eldest son was my grandfather, Richard Vijayaratnam Nevins. My grandfather was educated at Hindu College in Jaffna in the north of Ceylon and Trinity College in Kandy, which was in the central part of the country. His father, Timothy, was principal and teacher at both schools.

Vijayam passed out as a medical doctor in 1918. As was the custom of that time, his marriage was arranged. As part of that arrangement, Alfred Lawton funded Vijayam's passage and tuition to obtain his FRCS in Edinburgh in Scotland. My grandfather returned from Scotland and then married my grandmother Louisa in February 1928.

As I reflect on the wonderful atmosphere in that large house, I wonder how much of that made a difference to who I became. When you are growing up as a child you are absorbing things at a terrific rate. If the basic needs such as the physiological needs, safety, love and belonging are there one can begin at an early age to absorb the concepts of self-confidence, of leadership, of ethics. I grew up in a house full of people with leadership traits and humility. They were quiet achievers. I find it hard to believe that some of that did not rub off on me growing up in this house.

My father had just starting his working life. Young graduate engineers working for the government barely made much money. He started with a salary of Rs 500 a month. Living with the extended family, with his In-Laws, yet having his own space for the family in a separate unit was of great benefit. My grandparents had the domestic help and were cooking most meals. Lunch was always the main meal and we would share that as a large family, but my mother would always prepare dinner. Even with this help, my father found it a struggle to live within his wages. He took to lecturing on telecommunications at the Katubede campus and the Peradeniya campus of the university to supplement his income.

I am mindful of the need to appreciate that the choices and hard work of the previous generation, such as Alfred Lawton, Timothy Nevins Selvadurai, Gunam and Emily Watson, and my grandfather and grandmother, Vijayam and Louisa, enabled us to live comfortably in our own home closer to the centre of Colombo. If my father had used part of his salary for the renting of a home, he would have lived much further away. He may have not afforded to send both me and my sister to private schools.

My nursery school was not far from home. I was three. A new way of teaching young children had emerged called the Montessori Method. This method encourages self-direction in learning for young children. Classes can be mixed with all ages, and individuals play and learn with the items that interest them. Joyce Goonesekera ran the school at Charles Circus, a kilometre from our home. Joyce was taught by the founder of this method, Dr. Maria Montessori. I was enrolled and started my education with "Aunty Joyce."

White shirt and blue shorts, that was the uniform of my first school, a school also not far from home, a school by the coastal railway line and the sea in Colpetty, St. Thomas' Preparatory School. As its name suggests, it was the junior school of the St. Thomas' College at Mount Lavinia a good 10 Km to the south along the coast. The classes at prep went up to standard five after which you went to the senior school or to another college.

My grandfather died when I was eleven years old. He was seventy-four. There are some events in one's life that clearly leave a scar. Events that changed your view of the world in which you had such a small influence. Events that changed a comfort you had hoped would be forever. My grandfather was the patriarch in this close knit family and a huge influence in this house. He fell ill with cancer of the pancreas that was detected about a year before he died. He loved his job as surgeon at the Ratnam's private hospital and operated and cured patients till the age of seventy-three. He was a huge influence in my life.

My memories of him clearly are dimming with age but I can still recall his dark tall handsome figure and his warm smile.

My grandfather was a chain smoker. He used to carry a Du Maurier tin of cigarettes in his hand all the time. Each tin had fifty cigarettes and he used to finish a tin in a day. I was fascinated by the respect he commanded and this leadership was not just within the family but also the community. SJV Chelvanayagam was the leader of the main political party representing the Tamil language speaking people. The party was called the Federal Party and their main electorate was in the North of Ceylon. SJV as he was known was being treated for his Parkinson's by my grandfather. He would visit my grandfather and spend evenings discussing the political events of the day. My grandfather was interested and discussed intently but never got involved in politics.

As a young child spending time with him was special. Even as a young boy I was aware of the respect he commanded by anyone and everyone who knew him. I still have vivid memories of the funeral and the large crowds that attended to pay their respects. His passing away had a profound impact on my sister and my cousin Surendran and me. This was the first death of a member of that wonderful extended family. We lost our first grandparent and one who we had spent so much time with. We both were supportive of our grandmother at the funeral walking beside her, two eleven-year-olds pretending to somehow make her loss bearable. As I reflect now, I realise what a legacy he had left behind. So many people owed the extension of their lives due to the skills he had as a surgeon. He had healed so many; they were grateful and had come to pay their respects.

Vijayam completed his FRCS in Edinburgh in Scotland, and his first posting as a surgeon in the Colonial Health Service was in Matale. After Matale, and his marriage to my Grandmother he was posted to Trincomalee, during his time here in 1929, his first child, a daughter, Christine, was born in Colombo. Following his first posting to Trincomalee, he had many postings to various towns in

Ceylon. One such posting was to Badulla in central Ceylon. Badulla had a cool climate, and the town was surrounded by lush tea estates. It was while he was here that his second child, also a daughter, Irene, my mother, was born. He delivered my mother at the home of his father-in-law, Alfred Lawton, in Colombo.

Following his various postings in Kurunegala and Galle around 1940 he was posted to Colombo. Here in Colombo, he was confronted with a choice. He was confronted with a life and death choice. A decision to be made instantly, a choice that would change his life and the life of his patient.

This was one of those moments in one's life where status quo, not doing anything was also a choice, an acceptable option. One of those moments where making the choice with risks had consequences for one's career. At Colombo General Hospital, he was confronted with this patient who had been just stabbed and the knife had pierced the heart.

Thoracic surgery was in the early 1940s restricted to the confines of the exterior of the chest. Intra thoracic procedures were not feasible and not done. Cardiac surgery not thought of. The first closed heart operation in Ceylon was done years later in 1952 by Professor Husfeldt of Denmark. No one in Ceylon had opened the chest and sutured the heart.

No one would have blamed him if he had not taken the risk. Posterity does not record the times that one does not make the choice. The patient would have been a statistic forgotten except by his close relatives. But his choice was to take the risk and try to save this person's life. Vijayam that day with no previous experience to count on, no expert to refer to, opened up and sutured the heart of this patient. He never boasted about this historical operation.

It was left to others who later credited him with performing the first cardiac operation in Ceylon.

A serious accident on the way to his father's funeral may have altered my story.

Vijayam and the family were holidaying in Nuara Eliya, a hill station in central Ceylon. The cool climate of Nuara Eliya made it a favourite holiday destination of the British. The town resembled a village in England. While on holiday there, he received the news that his father had passed away in Jaffna in the north of Ceylon. As his father was an eminent person in the community, a former member of the state legislature, the funeral was to be a significant event. As the eldest male in the family he had to be there. There was a lack of embalming facilities during that era, and the funeral had to take place soon.

Vijayam took the family his wife Louisa, and daughters Christine and Irene in the Austin car that he had at that time. Their driver drove for a number of hours and Vijayam decided to relieve the driver. Vijayam was a very fast driver, and near Madawachiya on the road to Jaffna, the car spun off the road and overturned. Vijayam was bleeding from the neck, there were other serious injuries to others in the car, but luckily no one required hospitalisation. After attending to their wounds, they took the train and continued their journey to attend the funeral.

Even when there is nothing to divide us, we humans find some way of differentiating ourselves from others. There was a distinction made between those who got their FRCS in Edinburgh and those who got it in London. Vijayam had a difference in opinion about the next appointment. He decided that instead of getting too involved in the hospital appointment politics, he would take a six-month furlough to Europe with my grandmother Louisa. He would think about his future after he returned.

As he was making his plans to travel to Europe, Hitler invaded Poland and started what was to be the Second World War. It was not safe to go to Europe.

Vijayam decided to go and see his sister in Malaya, instead. My grandmother was happy at this change of plan. The planned trip to Europe meant leaving the two daughters in boarding at the school they attended called Ladies College. When the trip to Europe was cancelled and the destination changed to Klang in Malaya, she insisted she was not going without her two girls. Vijayam, Louisa, Christine, and Irene—the whole family at that time—went by ship for what they thought was a six-month holiday.

Japan got involved in the war. Singapore, the capital of Malaya, fell and the British retreated. The family got stuck in a Japanese-occupied Malaya for five years.

My mother talks fondly about this time in her life. It was at that time, at her age, such an adventure. The world was at war, but for her and elder sister Christine, it was an opportunity to spend quality time with their father. In Ceylon, as a surgeon, in the various hospitals he was posted in, he was busy, on call, dedicated to his work. Here, stuck in Malaya during the war he would tutor them during the day as there was no school.

After a while, the tutoring got a bit too much. They welcomed the Allied bombing. She relates how they would wait for the air-raid siren warning about the bombs about to drop so they could get into the shelter and avoid the tuition.

The Japanese paraded the British soldiers and the key administrators they had captured in the streets, humiliating them and getting the locals to watch. My mother recalls that when they heard that the army was approaching up the streets in Klang, they would run and hide. The army was known to randomly capture and rape women in the town. Dr. Hoisington, their uncle, who they were staying with, was imprisoned by the Japanese for treating the injured retreating British soldiers. The Japanese needed him to treat their own injured and sick soldiers and released him later.

There was no communication possible during that time between Malaya and Ceylon because of the war. The news in Ceylon was that the Japanese having taken Singapore were advancing north of Malaya. They were taking British soldiers as prisoners. The family in Colombo thought the worst had happened—that my grandfather and family had died in the war.

The six-month holiday turned out to be an adventure too long for even the young Christine and Irene.

The war abruptly ended for those in Malaya. They were not aware of the bombing of Hiroshima and Nagasaki and the subsequent surrender of Imperial Japan to the Allies on August 15, 1945. The British took their time getting back to the colonies. As the British had not arrived yet and the Japanese had lost control, looting and revenge attacks were widespread in the country. The British returned to find Malaya and the capital, Singapore, in bad shape. Food and medical facilities were dangerously low. Allied bombing had taken its toll. Electricity, gas, water, and telephone facilities were in serious disrepair.

In this chaotic environment, the family tried their best to get out. They decided the best option was to first get to the capital Singapore. They boarded a train from Klang to Singapore. Unfortunately, many others had the same idea. The train was packed to the brim.

Allied bombing had also destroyed Singapore harbour facilities, and numerous wrecks blocked the harbour. There was no way to get back to Ceylon by ship. My grandfather somehow persuaded the administration in this chaotic situation to allow his family to get on one of the rare flights out of Singapore to Colombo.

The rest of the family were delightfully surprised when they returned back to Ceylon, not four of them but five, a new addition to the family, my aunt Kamala.

Ceylon like most Asian societies was very family oriented. Colombo like some of the other colonial capitals had a vibrant social scene. The clubs around sports such as rugby and cricket being the main meeting place after the day's work. The pace of life was slower. There was no television. As an extended family, we met regularly at each other's house. The birthday of a cousin, aunt, or uncle was a great excuse. It was tradition to drop in on the family celebrating. This was a chance for the whole family to get together, sharing some finger food and a drink.

Even as a young boy I frequented the Ceylon Lawn Tennis Association club, which was quite close to my home. I was coached and started playing tennis from an early age. I was taken there most days not by my parents but my grandfather's brother. AJDN.

Arthur Joseph Devanayagam Nevins Selvadurai, AJDN, or Selva to his many friends, was simply Devanayagam Uncle to me. By choice he was a bachelor. He had a sportsman's trot as he walked more on his toes. He was tall and fit and someone who was amazingly comfortable with himself. He was so contented. He was a lawyer, but hardly charged anyone for his services. He drove an old car that had holes in the floorboards. He never yearned for the better car. He lived with the minimum of furniture. He never yearned for his own home or fancy furnishings. I never knew of his sporting feats growing up. He never talked about it.

The schools had a very special place in the social structure of Colombo society in Ceylon. They still do. Two of the oldest schools are Royal College and St. Thomas' College. Cricket is the national sport of Sri Lanka. A combination of these two passions, school and cricket, has spurned the second longest annual cricket encounter in the world. The battle of the blues. The battle of the blues has been running for over 133 years and has the unique record of continuing even through both World Wars I and II. Chosen to play in this unique match meant you had a special place in history.

Selva as he was known in school was an all-rounder, an opening bowler and an early order batsman. He represented St. Thomas' College at cricket from 1927 to 1929. There are some classic tales that demonstrated his prowess with the bat and ball. One was his innings against Wesley College where he scored 144, which included 32 runs in one over. He bludgeoned five sixes and one four, the umpire C.V Corke a master of college ruled one of the sixes a four and so the score was recorded as 32. The other legend is that he hit a six during a match at St. Thomas's ground, which is adjacent to the railway line and the sea. The ball landed inside a passing train and the ball was carried all the way several miles away to the town of Panadura.

One story, though, captures the spirit of a bygone era, captures the gentlemanly qualities in him and those of his generation.

It was the Royal-Thomian of 1929. Royal had thoroughly dominated the Thomians and had twenty runs to make in their second innings with about ten minutes of play left. Today, teams would delay proceedings and would not give any opportunity for the opposition to make the required runs. Selva belonged to another era.

The Thomians ran onto the field. Selva and Roy Herman, the captain of St. Thomas's, opened the bowling. Royal made the required runs.

Selva was to relate later that they decided to give Royal every chance of winning the game. Though they were both fast bowlers, between Roy Herman and him, they bowled six overs in ten minutes. It was a sport to all of them of that generation. They played it as such.

Selva played for many years for the Tamil Union cricket club as their opening bowler. He also played for Ceylon when the overseas teams visited the island on their way to England or Australia. He played for All-Ceylon against the Australians led by Lindsay Hasset. The team included Keith Miller. He opened the bowling for Ceylon and scored thirty-six. I learnt of all of this much later in life.

I can't imagine after spending so much time with him while growing up there was no influence on me. As a leader, it is important to have a sense of justice and fair play, not to favour one over others. I am acutely aware that I have this sense of giving people the benefit of the doubt, not judging too quickly, listening to both sides of the story. However thinly you slice salami, there are always two sides. I would like to think it came from AJDN.

I attended St. Thomas' Preparatory School in Colombo and then moved to St. Thomas' College in Mount Lavinia. They were both schools by the sea. Several of my grand-uncle's including AJDN, DJN, BSN Selvadurai had attended this school and excelled in sports. All of them had different records to their names. Many other uncles of the next generation of Selvadurai's DDN, PSN had also attended and excelled in sports, playing cricket for the School.

DDN Selvadurai had played in the seventy-fifth Royal Thomian cricket encounter in 1953. It was a match captained by Ian Peiris, and the Thomians had won convincingly that year beating Royal by an innings and thirty-four runs. He was around twenty years older to me, and had left school when I had begun my schooling at Prep. DDN, went on to be a National Tennis champion and Davis Cup player. His younger brother Paul Selvadurai played in the Royal Thomian cricket encounter in 1962. I was seven years old and at St. Thomas Prep school and remember being taken for the match at the Colombo Oval. The family had a unique record. Their father, Doraj Selvadurai, had played for Royal College in 1918. The father and two sons playing for the two opposing schools in this historical cricket series.

My father attended this school as did all of his six brothers. A couple of them had won academic prizes. I was a third generation, Thomian. I had a tough act to follow.

I neither won any academic prize nor excelled in any sport. I played tennis for the college and represented the college at athletics. I was a chorister in the chapel choir. My academic record was ordinary.

St Thomas College was steeped in tradition and is over 150 years old. It was founded during the British rule of Ceylon by the first Anglican Bishop of Colombo the Rev. James Chapman. It was modelled on Eton College in England. We are all influenced by the school we attend. It's a living breathing experience, the teachers of the time, your friends and classmates. We spend so much time, in school, at the stage of our lives that we are absorbing more than just the education the school provides. I have come to appreciate the sacrifices my parents made to send me to STC. Although an ordinary student, it provided me a well-rounded education, discipline, and friends for life.

I was a rebel in my teens. I smoked whenever I could afford it. Today, I have two spots in my lungs that are not malignant but are a trophy of my smoking days. I gave up smoking at twenty-one, and I have not touched a cigarette since. I occasionally smoke a cigar.

We played truant from School during our teens. After marking the class register as being present, Christians would have to attend a daily short service in the chapel before the classes began. The non-Christians would be playing a quick game of cricket outside. It was an opportune time to sneak away by mingling with the non-Christians, take a train from the railway station at Mount Lavinia, and travel to Colombo. We would either watch a movie or go the American Centre at Galle Face Court where we would listen to Jimi Hendrix and read books. They were carefree days but a dangerous time for me, I could have drifted down a slippery path of no return. Choices in my life were very limited at that age, I was still under the watchful eye of my parents, but the few choices I had, could be dangerous. Moving from cigarettes to drugs would have been an easy step. I didn't make that choice.

One morning, we were happily walking to the railway station, having just played truant from school. We were all smoking. Unfortunately for us, there were also some seniors, including college prefects, in the same vicinity, close to the entrance of the Mount Lavinia Hotel, who spotted us. They too were smoking. We got caught. They were not pleased that we juniors had seen them.

The next few days were extremely stressful. I had not thought of the consequences of my truancy and of getting caught. I had hidden this side of my life from my parents. As a young boy, I was nervous and not knowing what to expect. Our main punishment was six lashings of the bamboo cane by the highest authority in the school, the warden. We only just avoided the next level of punishment, which would have been a suspension. The principal or head teacher of St. Thomas' College was called the warden. Mr. Anandanayagam was an elderly gentlemen who had been a physics teacher for many years and was now the warden. He had taught my father. He knew the family well.

Even at his age, he was known for the strength of his arm in delivering a lashing on your buttocks with the bamboo cane. Why it was six lashings and not four or five I never knew. It was always six. Sitting in the reception area of the warden's office, nervously awaiting your call for this one-to-one with the warden was stressful. You had to mentally prepare yourself for this beating. Your name is called. The warden exchanged some pleasantries, chit chat, before he asked you to bend and hold his desk. His arm would then wind in a swing similar to a baseball batsman and *whack*! You feel a stinging pain in your buttocks before the pain spreads. Before you can recover the next one. Six times this was repeated. You had to be brave; you could not cry. The pain was reaching your brain.

That official punishment was preceded by torture in the prefect's room. The prefects deliberated if they were going to escalate this case to the warden. As they deliberated, they made us chew and eat cigarettes, stand on one leg, and other silly tasks. They decided to escalate.

Of course, none of this compared to the humiliation I felt when the school called my parents in to report and discuss the incident. This was a part of my life my parents were not aware of. It came as a complete shock to them. The guilt and the realisation of the hurt I had caused them continued for a few weeks.

As part of my rehabilitation, I was asked to attend special classes after school with Rev. Townsend, the rector of the school. Rev. Townsend was a rotund Australian priest. These classes were to prepare me for confirmation in the college chapel. Confirmation marks the point in the Christian journey at which you affirm for yourself the faith into which you have been baptized and your intention to live a life of committed discipleship. This affirmation is confirmed through prayer and the laying on of hands by the confirming bishop. I had been baptised a Methodist; I was only attending these classes to appease my parents. I knew this was part of my punishment for what I had done.

My father was a very stern and strong person and about that time became the central figure in my life determining and creating the environment that would shape my choices for the rest of my life. I was young and restless. He was a strong anchor, he was patient. He tactfully guided me; he understood that he needed to give me space to discover my independence. He understood keeping too tight a leash meant I could rebel to such an extent that it would be detrimental to my life and my future.

Many things were happening at that time. You could also say I was moving from my mother's influence and protection that I always enjoyed to understanding that I had to now deal with my father directly without the mediation of my mother. Later, I appreciated that my father was flying blind. He had lost his father very early in life and had no model of fatherhood or parenting to follow. Today, I am eternally grateful for whatever he did to control that rebel teenager; it could have been a different story today, if not for his love.

Growing up, my world revolved around my extended family living in these conjoined houses, my school and my friends living just outside the gates of my home. As I grew older, I drifted out of the house and into the street. Street cricket was the initial draw.

There were many boys and girls living down Unity Place, Inner Flower Road and 28th Lane. We drifted into friendship. No one introduced us. All of us were approximately the same age, the only common factor being that we loved playing cricket and were part of this neighbourhood.

As we grew older together the relationships became stronger. It went beyond just the love of playing street cricket. We moved out together outside the neighbourhood as a group. The "drain gang" became our identity.

There was a large drain running the length of Unity Place. It was covered in most parts by a concrete cover, but exposed at the end of the street.

During the monsoon when we would have heavy floods, the street would be more like a river—the drain being unable to cope with the volume of water—and all of the boys down the street would be out wading and splashing in the muddy water.

The remarkable thing about the drain gang is the enduring relationship that has stood the test of time and distance. All of us are still good friends, despite the fact that we are spread around the world. Despite the fact that we may have not met for years, there is an instant rapport, no awkwardness, when we meet. We don't need to take time to catch up. It's instant. It's electric and often the envy of any outsider in our midst.

We were different. We were from all the different communities living in Ceylon and then Sri Lanka, Sinhalese, Tamil, Burgher, Christian, Buddhist, Muslim, and Hindu. Our parents were not great mates, just the usual passing greeting to a neighbour. Yet we had a bond that never called into question our differences. We celebrated our common denominator, which was the fact that we were in this secluded, quiet neighbourhood, we enjoyed each other's company, and we enjoyed playing cricket on the street. We were both boys and girls, protective of each other and suspicious of the intruders into our street.

"In life we never lose friends, we only learn who our true friends are". One true friend in our gang was Puji. He was confident as a teenager, had more freedom from his parents than most of us, was able to appear aggressive and yet he would be the most concerned if anything happened to anyone of us. You could be confident he would always be there for you. I spent a lot of time with Puji growing up and we got up to some crazy things together.

As we grew and our interest in girls changed from being just mates to puppy love, this grew into having a special girlfriend, breaking up, and falling in love again. The girls' schools were a big attraction for the teenage boys with hormones running wild. Anytime there was an event such as a fundraising fair, carnival, or concert, it was a good time to spruce up and meet the girls. A few of us now are married to the friends we met at this time.

We organised many parties, mainly as a pretext to meet the girls— low lights, slow music, and some cheap booze. None of us can hide our past from each other; it provides a grounding, a reality check. There is no pretence to be anything more than who you are, all of us just members of this close, neighbourhood gang, a group of friends who have a very special and unique relationship.

The Beatles were making waves in the music scene, and their songs played on the radio. We had our own rock band in Ceylon who were called the Savages. Raj Seniviratne was the lead singer and guitar player. We admired their talent. Raj and Dalrene Arnolda, together with the Savages, toured Vietnam during the war, entertaining the US troops. I was thrilled to meet Raj much later in life. He is not in the best of health, however, has his own music studio and only does work when he wants to. He helped to compose and play on some of the advertising radio jingles for Mobitel.

Around the same time, we also had a group called the Bugs, another rock band, with frontman Kumar (Baba) Navaratnam. He was also a legend and genius on the electric guitar. I had the pleasure of meeting him too, in the '90s. He is now living in the USA.

The tickets for the concerts were not cheap. We would beg, borrow, or steal to find the money for the tickets. Many times, we just breached the security and sneaked in by jumping over fences to get to the concert and listen to the music.

I had another interest at this time, which was tennis. I played regularly and made many new friends who were not from the neighbourhood and not from my school. There was a national circuit for tennis tournaments, and we would travel by bus and train to Galle, Nuwara Eliya, Badulla, and Jaffna for their local club tournaments. The nationals were always held every year at Colombo at my club, the CLTA. The public schools tournament was also held every year at the same club. One year we did particularly well. My doubles partner, Arj, and I, representing our school, St. Thomas' College, were the runners-up of the tournament.

I was sixteen years old when I was exposed to a violent, fatal crime that I had never envisaged possible in my protected world. I attended a private school and lived in a relatively sheltered neighbourhood. My exposure to the world outside this sheltered life would be the bus ride to school and back every day. Colombo was a peaceful and safe city. The busses were old double-deckers that had been imported from London Transport. The busses were relatively clean and not crowded. I usually got a seat on the upper deck of the route 106 or 134 from Flower Road to my school in Mount Lavinia. Things were orderly and disciplined. It was a different world to the Colombo of today.

The first and deep cut to my protected glass world happened on that fateful day in 1971. To me, this was the beginning of the end of the paradise in which I had been living, this world where the members of every community lived harmoniously in our neighbourhood, this world where my parents would not worry if I was out late chatting to my friends on the street, this world where any home invasion and certainly any murder would have made the front pages of the newspapers.

This crack appeared just before the dark time in the history of the country, just before the youth in the south of the island started an insurgency that saw the birth of the JVP. The country would later see the birth of the LTTE that dragged this paradise further to the depths of hell. Before all of those events that eventually made killing and murder an everyday occurrence in Colombo, my innocence was confronted with the murder of my father's brother, my uncle Sextus.

It was the weekend. The government had changed the weekend from the usual Saturday and Sunday for political gain. The new weekend was based on the cycles of the moon. The weekends were called a pre-Poya and Poya day. One of the Poya days would coincide with the full moon every month.

I recalled it was a Poya day, a day when it was customary for Buddhists go to the temple for prayer and meditation. It was a quiet day with hardly any traffic on the roads. "Emilstan" was at 469 Galle Road, close to the Galle Road and Bullers Road junction at the entrance to Temple Lane in the suburb of Bambalapitiya. This was the home of my father's mother, my grandmother Emily.

Emily was very special to me. My father would let me spend a few days here every school holiday since I was six years old, and I had happy memories of the house and the time spent with my grandmother and the two uncles who lived there. Emily was a remarkable woman, quiet but inwardly strong and confident of herself. I did not know then what risks she had taken and the choices she had made to be a single parent, to bring up seven boys on her own, after the death of her husband.

I recall we would sit together, just the two of us on the veranda of this house, and she would inquire about my world. She would be amused at my observations and stories. She was quiet, yet you could sense her inner strength, her confidence, her wisdom. Two of my father's brothers, Sextus and Dalton, were bachelors at that time and lived with their mother, Emily.

Sextus was a successful solicitor. He had a home office in addition to his chambers at Hulsdorf near the courts. He was a very tidy person, and everything on his desk in his office was neatly in place. As a child, I would wander in there, fascinated, wanting to draw or use his pens and pencils. He was never harsh, but you knew he was annoyed if things were not in place. He always had sweets in his drawer for me. As part of his work, he would hold cash in trust for clients, maybe as part of a property transaction or other matter.

Dalton was a nutrition expert. He had found a job in Ghana and had gone overseas. This just left Emily and Sextus alone in the house. A relative who normally would come down from Kandy and use their home as a base for his work in Colombo was not well and did not turn up that week. Emily and Sextus woke up on that fateful day and went about having their early morning cup of tea.

Two persons knocked on the gate that sits behind a bus stop on Galle Road. Normally a busy road with people waiting for their bus, it was quiet. A male domestic cleaner, who would normally open the gate, was away due to the holiday. Sextus opened the gate and recognised that one of the two standing there was a male domestic helper of one of his clients. They had a letter for him. He let them into the hallway inside the main door. This was barely fifteen feet from the main road and the normally busy bus stand. As they entered the hallway, the two men pushed him down and stabbed him violently several times. He had no inkling of his fate; he was caught unawares, and his last words were to shout a warning to his mother.

Emily, hearing the warning, had run and hid in the servant's toilet at the back of the house. She stayed there many hours, not knowing when it was safe or the fate of her son, Sextus. Eventually she emerged and alerted a neighbour who discovered the body and called my father.

I was preparing for my ordinary-level exam. We had prepared and sat for the exam in December 1970, but the exam papers were leaked. We had to re-sit the exam in March. I was attending tuition classes on that Poya day weekend. After the class, which was conducted not far from Emily's home, I usually dropped in to see her and keep her company. I had no idea what had happened. There were no mobile phones or ways of keeping in touch. I walked in to the home expecting the usual greeting from my grandmother. It was eerily quiet.

One cannot imagine, at the age of sixteen, the level of emotional shock that one can get, being confronted by the body of someone close to you, violently stabbed and covered in blood, the limbs twisted at an awkward angle. There was no television in those days, none of the murder visuals we see every day now. It was confronting. I just stared at the still and bloodied body of my uncle Sextus, his eyes still wide open in shock. The police had yet to arrive, and my father was busy comforting his very distressed mother.

The domestic and his accomplice, aware that there was a property transaction in progress, wrongly assumed that there would be cash in my uncle's office. They ransacked the office and left it in a mess. They consumed his whiskey. They stepped over his body and left without much cash. They were clumsy. They had left clues behind.

My grandmother never recovered from that incident; her life seemed a little less worth living. I was always aware that from that day there was a difference in her, a little less spark, a sadness in her eyes. We never worked out if she had witnessed anything that fateful day.

She never spoke about it. She never harboured any hate for the accused, who were caught, tried, and convicted.

I admire her now. I know more about her life now than I knew then. She was a woman who had lost her husband early in life, had lost her only daughter also early in life, had been the only one in the house during this murder of one of her sons. She had singlehandedly brought up seven boys. I admire her as she had always drawn on an inner strength, her faith and her sense of duty to the sons she so loved.

I completed my ordinary-level exams. The results were not at the top end of the scale. I had passed. For someone who was always challenged academically in school, the results were something to be proud of.

Even more fractures were appearing in my paradise. Fractures that over my lifetime ripped the country apart, north and south, rich and poor, capitalist and Marxist, Sinhalese and Tamil, Muslim and Buddhist. The dawn of terrorism had arrived to this island paradise.

The world too was in turmoil. In March 1971, the Pakistan army launched a military operation against students, civilians, and armed personnel in East Pakistan. These Bengalis had demanded the Pakistan military junta accept the 1970 election results, which were won by an Eastern Pakistan party. The war in Bangladesh had begun.

The war in Vietnam was raging between North Vietnam, supported by the communists of the Soviet Union and China, and South Vietnam, supported by the United States and other anti-communist countries.

Kim Il Sung, a communist, was the leader of North Korea. North Korea was as prosperous as the South.

In 1971, Rohana Wijeweera was twenty-eight years old. His father was an active member of the communist party. There were two communist parties at that time in Ceylon. One was the Soviet wing, and the other was the Chinese wing. Rohana's father belonged to the Soviet wing. Eleven years earlier, when he was seventeen and at a time when it was extremely rare to travel overseas, Rohana won a scholarship to study medicine at the Lumumba University in Moscow. He returned three years later, after he contracted an illness, and joined the Chinese wing of the communist party. The acrimony between the two wings of the communist parties were such that he was not allowed to return to Russia.

Rohana was about to inflict the first and most shocking blow to this island paradise.

Rohana had secretly over the preceding five years been forming a movement called the *Janatha Vimukthi Peramuna*, or JVP. It was an organisation based on the Marxist doctrine that Rohana cleverly broke into the five lectures, lectures he conducted throughout the country. The so-called "Five Lectures" included discussions of Indian imperialism, the growing economic crisis, the failure of the island's communist and socialist parties, and the need for a sudden, violent seizure of power. The group funded themselves by conducting armed robberies and armed themselves by making home-made bombs. Youth my age of sixteen and older were being recruited into the movement. Young policemen and soldiers were also recruited. They were all given navy-blue uniforms and home-made weapons. Training was secretly held in the remote jungles of Ceylon.

The youth in the south were disillusioned with many things but mainly the lack of employment opportunities. The economy was in the doldrums. Globally, too, things were not good. In April that year, they struck, attacking and capturing ninety-three of the 273 police stations in the country.

The government of Mrs. Srimavo Bandaranaike was totally unprepared for this insurrection. A period of dusk to dawn curfew was imposed. Our lives, all changed. The middle-class bubble that we were living in, a bubble whose existence we were not aware of, burst. We were totally disconnected from the aspirations and frustrations of the youth outside Colombo.

Violence and the random killing of fellow humans entered the culture of Sri Lanka. The element of surprise gave the insurgents the upper hand in the initial few months. The armed forces regrouped. The government sought the help of the Indian government and Pakistan, who sent in troops and helicopters to guard essential installations, such as airports, and to patrol the coast. The violence was given back in full measure by the armed forces and police in the same year. Thousands of young men and women died and were buried in unmarked graves. This was a turning point for this paradise island. The politicians became thugs. Thugs became politicians.

My life changed too. Completing the ordinary-level exams was like a rite of passage. Compared with the options that young sixteen-year-olds have today, my choices were very limited. But I had a choice, a choice that had to be made with the support of my parents.

I could stay in school and pursue my advanced-level studies in Tamil, which was the entrance exam for the local university. Most of my fellow students continued in school, following the advanced-level classes and completing the exam before making their choices about what to do next.

I could stay in school and attend tuition classes outside school hours and at weekends to pursue my advanced-level studies in English, sit for the London advanced-level exams. This gave you options for university overseas. There were some students who took that option.

My choice was completely different. I left school. I took the option of doing the London advanced level, but I also enrolled in a diploma of technology apprenticeship course.

I had a different reason to quit school early. I struggled in my studies as my schooling was in my ancestral language of Tamil. My natural language, or "mother tongue," was English. I had spoken only English at home. I thought in English. I translated every word in my head as one would do when speaking and reading a foreign language. Having completed the ordinary-level exams in Tamil, I was free to pursue my next level of studies in English. I left school and did it privately.

My parents were supportive. I was at the age where I had absolutely no understanding of what these choices meant. I was excited about getting out of the school system.

In May 1972, Ceylon became the Free and Independent Republic of Sri Lanka. That year, I entered the technical college in Moratuwa. Moratuwa was further south along the Galle Road from Colombo, even further than my school at Mount Lavinia, a longer bus ride for me from my home in Kollupitiya.

It is hard to imagine today how this choice I made was very different to the choices being made by my classmates at St. Thomas' College. The norm was for everyone to complete their schooling by doing the advanced-level exam and then making choices after those results were known. University places in Sri Lanka were very limited. It was extremely competitive. Yet most students chose to stay and complete their advanced level in school. Once the results were known, they made their choices in pursing further studies.

My father was a visiting lecturer at the engineering campus of the university in Moratuwa. Linked to the university was the technical college. My father was aware of the diploma in technology course being run by the college. Since I had finished my O levels, I had the qualifications and could enter this course.

I was looking forward to this new experience, leaving school, studying in English.

Education was free. The problem was that tertiary education had not developed to keep pace with the number of students completing their advanced-level exams. The competition for the few places available in universities was fierce. You could have struggled to study, with no electricity in your home, your parents poor and sacrificing everything to get you educated. You receive good results but could not get a place in the university. This was a situation in the country that Rohana Wijeweera and the JVP exploited.

The technical college was the only tertiary institution in the whole country offering a diploma that included a six-month apprenticeship in its three-year curriculum. The competition to get into this course was also very stiff. Students applied from all parts of the island. Only a few were selected. Most students would aspire to get to university first. This was a second choice. Many of the students entering the technical college had already completed their advanced-level exams. They were older than me.

I was seventeen and had grown up in a much protected world. All the classmates in my school and friends and neighbours came from similarly privileged backgrounds. We had grown up in Colombo with Western music. I had watched the film *Woodstock* many times. We had Hollywood movie stars as our heroes. We were captivated by the freedom expressed in movies like *Easy Rider*.

We were not exposed to the struggle of the rest of the country and the reasons Rohana Wijeweera found such a large following to start a revolution in the country a year before.

The clash of our two worlds for me and the few Colombo schoolboys joining the course was like the confluence of two rivers joining in a flash flood.

There was a tradition in universities particularly in the subcontinent countries of India, Pakistan, and Sri Lanka, where "freshers," or the new entrants in a year, were "ragged" by the seniors. Sri Lanka over time developed a reputation as having the worst excess of ragging globally. Many students have died.

Two weeks into the ragging at the Katubedde campus, I was wishing I was dead.

It was the most humiliating, degrading experience for this middle-class, protected boy. An English-speaking, stuck-up, Colombo private-school boy was easy meat. I dreaded making that long bus journey from Colombo to Moratuwa every morning only to be dragged out and ragged; it was hell.

It made me grow up very fast. It made me stronger. These were all boys and girls older than me. Yet I realised that I had a confidence and self-belief that they lacked. I relied on that to give me strength.

In this turmoil and stress, I met Mario. He was from a similar background to me, we became friends and helped each other through the ragging and the diploma course.

I was suddenly exposed to the real Sri Lanka. The youth, many from the rural parts of Sri Lanka, had fewer opportunities, particularly in this economy, which was in deep recession. The ambition of all young people at that time was to get a degree and get a job in the government. The lack of enough universities meant they did not get there. Those who successfully did, and graduated, found there were no government jobs available.

Many of those who ragged me later became friends. A few of them were hard-core JVP. Others were sympathetic to the JVP views. We had many visits by police during lectures to pick students for questioning. Our year-end exam had a special enclosure for those who had been charged. They were brought in handcuffed and taken back after the exams.

We would greet them and acknowledge them before the exams commenced.

In May that year, the Criminal Justice Commission of five judges of the Supreme Court were appointed to try those involved in the insurrection of April 1971. The attorney general framed charges on four counts, including "conspiracy to overthrow the lawfully elected government and waging war against it," against forty-one suspects in the case of the JVP insurgency. Forty were actually charged.

While I continued attending the diploma course during the week, I attended private, tuition classes during the weekends to prepare for taking the London advanced-level exams.

My apprenticeship was organised at the Colombo Commercial Company. The CCC was an engineering company specialising in servicing the many tea factories and their machines. It was my first experience of working. I can rightfully say that I started at the bottom of the working ladder. I was a labourer, working on the lathe machines at the workshop in their Slave Island facility in Colombo. It was not far from my home. We were first given menial tasks, just sweeping and cleaning, observing the machine operators. We were then trained and assisted in making parts for tea factory machines every day. I looked with envy at the executives who were taken as management trainees. Some were Thomians, seniors from my old school. They definitely had better canteen facilities and wore smart white trousers and white shirts to work. I was in greasy overalls. We were not allowed to mix.

There were no safety goggles and a hot piece of metal shot into my eye one day. Luckily, I did not suffer permanent damage to my eyesight. The scar in my eye remains today. It's a permanent reminder to me of where I started my working life.

It was 1973. The socialist government of Mrs Srimavo Bandaranaike had nationalised private companies and restricted land ownership. Prices were rising, and there was a recession. The former prime minister, Dudley Senanayake, passed away that year. Long lines of people from all over the country came to pay respects to his body that lay in state at the parliament. He had held the PM post four times.

The government introduced the policy of standardization that year. This policy was introduced to rectify disparities created in university enrolment in Sri Lanka. With limited places available and the increasing number of students qualifying for access, any policy would affect someone in the community. In essence, the policy introduced an affirmative-action scheme to assist geographically disadvantaged students to gain tertiary education. The resultant benefits enjoyed by Sinhalese students also meant a significant fall in the number of Tamil students gaining entry into the Sri Lankan university.

Affected by this policy was a student four months older than me. He was based in the north of the country. He studied in the Tamil language and was affected by this standardization policy. In 1973, in response to the debates on standardization, he had already formed the Tamil New Tigers. He was eighteen. He was later to drag this paradise further into the abyss. His name was Velupillai Prabhakaran.

I was eighteen, restless, and confused. I was mingling with my colleagues on the lathe machine shop floor during the day and my privileged, middle-class friends in the evening and weekends. I had failed my first attempt at the London advanced-level examinations.

Life went on. Colombo was not aware or chose to ignore the rumbling lava beneath the surface. We were fascinated by the music of the Spitfires with Desmond De Silva on vocals. He could croon as well as Engelbert Humperdinck. The nightclubs like the Little Hut in Mount Lavinia or the Blue Leopard at the Orient Hotel in Colombo were favourite places to meet. We listened to Mignonne Fernando, who sang with the Jetliners. The Miss Sri Lanka contest was won that year by Shiranthi Wickremasinghe. Her brother was a classmate, a fellow Thomian. She represented the country at the Miss World contest in London that year. In 2005, she became the first lady, the wife of the president of Sri Lanka.

I continued to study for my second attempt at the London A-level exams. I was increasingly convinced that my life was not going to be at those lathe machines. I aspired to be in the white uniform of the management trainee.

I gave up the diploma course without completing it. The JVP had become an official political party, and the radicalisation of students continued in Katubedde. It was not the right atmosphere or place to be. The desire to get out of the country was now a seed planted. It was nurtured, and it grew with the increasingly hopeless situation in the country. The population had increased to 13 million. It had increased more than 60 percent since I had arrived from London on that ship in 1955.

The rumbling lava erupted in 1978. Rohana Wijeweera launched his second revolution. It erupted again in 1983 with the killing of thirteen soldiers and the responding racial riots of July that year.

Colombo was on fire. The Tigers had surfaced. The eruptions, killing, and mayhem continued for another thirty-six years till 2009.

Colombo in 1973 did not have many high-rise buildings. The tallest building was the Ceylico Office Tower in the heart of the city, with a rooftop restaurant called Akasa Kadey. A new five-star hotel was being built with eight floors on the Galle Road close to the residence of the prime minister, Temple Trees. The engineering firm responsible for the electrical and mechanical works was the Commercial Company. I got a job as a supervisor for the electrical wiring for the hotel. The hotel was to be managed by the Oberoi Hotel chain from India. Today the hotel is the Cinnamon Grand Hotel. The original building, slightly refurbished but having the original structure, still stands on the site.

It was my first job as a supervisor, a leader at such a young age. There were several of us as electrical supervisors, and we were all assigned teams of labourers and one or two qualified electricians. I was still eighteen. It was my first job in charge of a team, in charge of people. I had matured enough with my stint at the technical college to handle this task. Every morning, we would meet and be given tasks to be done that day. As each floor was being built and concrete poured, we would have to lay the electrical ducts through which wires would be pulled. We would lay and tie the plastic ducts to the reinforcing metalwork that was laid. We would have to be present during the pouring of the concrete, even at night.

I continued to study for my London advanced-level examinations during the weekends. I finally passed the exam. I applied to many universities in England. I thumbed through the brochures and pictures of the universities in Britain available in the British council library close to my place at work. I had built up expectations. I desperately wanted to get out of the country.

It was 1974. Receiving the letter of admission to the University of Salford was the most fantastic moment in my life at that time. Maybe it was time. My destiny called.

My father on his government salary could not afford to send me to the UK. We were asset rich but cash poor. Even if you had cash, you could not take it out of the country. The situation was grim. Food rationing for essential items such as rice, sugar, and lentils was in place. You had to take a card to the government-run CWE outlet to get your share of rations for the week. This paradise was crumbling.

My father borrowed the money for my trip and university fees from his two brothers, Dalton and Stanley. They had both worked overseas. My father, too, left Sri Lanka later, taking early retirement from the Department of Telecommunications and went to work in Malawi in southern Africa. Being there, he was able to repay the money borrowed from his brothers and pay for my education in the UK.

My ticket out of this dire situation in the country, my shot at an opportunity out there, was given to me. Even at that young age, I was aware of the sacrifices that had been made.

Chapter 3

Back to Blighty

It was early September 1974. I was nineteen going on twenty. The offer for a place at the University of Salford, close to the city of Manchester in the north-west of England, had arrived a few weeks ago. The first round of offers is made to students who had put their preferences for various courses at specific universities and had achieved the desired results. My cousin Surendran and several of my friends had their offers. They were on their way to London.

After sorting out those who are offered and those who accepted, a second round is offered. I had given up hope of getting a place. The University of Salford sent me that wonderful letter. They insisted that I arrive within a few weeks, to be there for registration, induction, and the start of the semester. The preparations to leave had to be rushed. I was fortunate that my birth in England gave me the right to a British passport.

Sri Lankan passport holders were not allowed to leave the country without an exit visa. An application for this visa had to be made, and it took time to be granted. The granting of this visa was at the discretion of the socialist government. My time at Katubedde, a hotbed of the JVP, could have been a cause for investigation.

I was leaving without much cash in my pocket. You were only allowed to leave the country with a few pounds sterling, for expenses. This was barely enough to get you a taxi from Heathrow to London at that time. I was so busy and rushed with the excitement of leaving I did not have time for the usual farewells to my friends and my close family. I just left.

I arrived in England, full of hope. I had built up this image of a country, the former colonial power, to be one that had its streets paved in gold. The only pictures I had seen were the ones in books. There was no television at that time, no reality check. Those pictures, it appears, were all taken in the summer, on a bright, sunny day.

My arrival in London and my subsequent train ride to Manchester was a blur. I was still in basking in the euphoria of having left Sri Lanka.

Globally, all countries, including the USA, were going through a recession. This was a period when there was an oil crisis, a steel crisis, and a stock market crash. The situation in England was particularly bad. The three-day week was a state of emergency imposed by conservative Prime Minister Edward Heath. This three-day week had come into force in January that year and was still in place when I arrived. I had no idea this was happening when I left Sri Lanka. This meant that commercial users of electricity were limited to three, specific, consecutive days' consumption of electricity. Offices and factories were forbidden to work longer hours on those days. Services deemed essential were exempted from these regulations. Electricity blackouts across the country were widespread. Unemployment was reaching a million. Inflation was high. Edward Heath was replaced as prime minister, and Harold Wilson of the Labour Party was prime minister when I arrived.

If London seemed a bit developed, then Manchester was about ten years behind. Salford, just outside the city outskirts, was ten years behind Manchester. I started to notice that the sun was not visible on most days. It was dark and grey. It was cold, not just cold but a particularly damp cold that made your body feel colder than the temperature indicates. I had grown up in a tropical environment and had not appreciated it. We hardly talked about the weather. The English talked incessantly about it.

Living in Ceylon, I had hardly noticed the sun and its warmth. I took it for granted. As I write, there is this song playing on the radio that captures this sentiment of only realising what you miss when it is no longer there. The song by the group Passenger goes like this:

"Only know the light when it's burning low. Only know the sun when it starts to snow. Only know you love her when you let her go."

Not long after I had arrived in the country, an even more serious threat had emerged. The IRA had taken the war to the mainland by bombing two pubs in Birmingham and in Guildford. In October, a few days after I arrived, the IRA had detonated two six-pound gelignite bombs at two pubs in Guildford, Surrey, southwest of London. The pubs were targeted because they were popular with British army personnel stationed at the barracks close by. Four soldiers and one civilian were killed whilst a further sixty-five were wounded.

The houses in Salford were old and draughty. Student accommodation was limited at the university and relatively expensive. I had thought I would find cheaper accommodation outside. The winter was cold. The only affordable accommodation was in some of these old houses where rooms were let out to students. Toilets were shared. I could not sleep at night, as it was so draughty and cold in these old houses. However, many layers of clothing I put on, the cold was severe.

There was no central heating at that time in those old houses. Electricity costs were prohibitive, and there were blackouts. The euphoria of coming to England was wearing off. Going back was not an option. The flight ticket back would be equivalent to a year's university fees. Unlike today, it was expensive to travel.

This was a great transition in my life. I had not realised how much that the love and protection my parents and the extended large family we had in Colombo had cocooned me. I had not realised what a protected life I had lead. I had this false notion that I was a man of this world. Away from my parents and friends, I was vulnerable. I was deeply hurt by the racist remarks, the whole attitude to the colour of my skin, the misunderstanding of the average northern Englishman to Asians.

It's very different now. But in the '70s it was tough. Since this was my decision to leave Sri Lanka and to make it here in England, I put up with the attitude and the hostility. I grew up quickly. I was on my own. I experienced loneliness and learnt how not to be overwhelmed by it. I grew over a period of time to be comfortable with myself. I could be alone in a crowded room and yet not be too conscious of it. It was not easy. I worked at it.

The University of Salford had been recently redeveloped. There were a number of new buildings, well heated. The halls of residence were also newly built and well heated. Initially, I would spend all day and the evenings in the university—in the heated buildings, library, or student union—only to return to my cold and damp digs to sleep. Although more expensive, I yearned for staying in the university halls of residence. I managed to secure a place. Any hope of saving money by staying in cheaper digs was dashed. I was conscious of the money this was costing my dad, but I just could not live in the accommodation that was available outside.

In the second year of my course, I decided to explore, once again, the option of getting a cheaper place to stay. I was conscious of the cost and my father's struggle to pay for my education and lodging. The depression and high unemployment meant there were no part-time jobs that were easily available. The first year of university was tough. Most drop outs happen in the first year. I just managed to scrape through my exams and pass.

Responding to an advertisement placed on one of the university notice boards, I walked to the Ellor Street housing estate. It was a short, twenty-minute walk from the university. What confronted me was a sixties housing scheme, a concrete jungle, large multistorey buildings. There was graffiti on the walls and a sense you were approaching a rough neighbourhood. I was not interested in living in this area. I continued walking on the Broadwalk towards the Salford shopping centre, resolved to ring and express my regret of not keeping the appointment.

This was when I spotted what looked like a brand-new church, built in sandstone with a black-slate roof. It looked like it had a garden walled on two sides and the church and rectory of the church on the other two sides. My appointment was to see a room available at the rectory of this church. This building seemed so out of place. It was like finding an oasis in the middle of this concrete desert. As I noticed that the rectory building was new, I decided to keep my appointment. I approached the rectory. I rang the buzzer and asked to speak to Mrs Wyatt. I did not realise it then, but this was a pivotal moment in my life. I met the Wyatt family for the first time.

Their third child was born in the house a few days earlier; she was called Sarah. They had two other children, Rachael and Daniel.

Rachael, recently passed to the other side, now at peace and without suffering, now an angel, an angel with God.

There are some meetings and moments in your life that you recall in great detail because the choices you made that day changed your life forever. This was such a meeting and moment.

My life was blessed that day, meeting David and Helen Wyatt, who became my parents in England. I realise today how blessed I was in life, not just to have a set of natural parents but then to get adopted into another family, have sisters and brothers, and have parents like David and Helen Wyatt.

The city of Salford was separated by the River Irwell from its much larger and better known city of Manchester. Salford was famous for its cotton and textile industry during the Industrial Revolution, but went into decline once those industries moved overseas. In the sixties, the slum-cleaning programme flattened the houses of Ellor Street, and concrete tower blocks of apartments were built for the citizens. In the recession of 1970s, the people of Ellor Street did particularly badly, and the majority were on welfare. The Wyatts embraced this situation, providing spiritual support and doing anything they could to make life bearable for the residents of this large estate that was at the heart of their parish. I witnessed in the Wyatts this sense of complete, selfless giving to everyone who lived in the area, regardless of their religion or race. Anyone who came to their door was welcomed and offered a meal and shelter if they needed it. They did this regardless of who they were.

They had an old van, and David would go out in the van and collect furniture and old newspapers from some of the other suburbs. He would recycle the newspapers. He would deliver furniture to those in need. I witnessed miracles many times. They would have identified some need for a family. We would discuss it. The next day, a call would come, or items they were looking for would appear on their doorstep. Many homeless would be at the table, sharing their meals.

I was privileged to be witnessing what I call true spirituality. My definition of spirituality is the selfless helping of your fellow human. They were the living example of it here in the deprived, underdeveloped part of Salford. It was a joy to watch them work. I could never do what they did. I had too much of a sense of self. But my time with them helped me to understand that I had to have some balance, that unless I was also helping my fellow humans as I pursue my selfish motives, I would never be contented. Today, I am who I am, my inner peace comes, because I learnt this vital lesson of balance from the Wyatts. They had a huge influence in the choices I made in my life.

Mr and Mrs Wyatt were from a middle-class family born and brought up in the rolling hills of Lancashire. They were well educated. David was educated at Cambridge University, where he obtained his PhD. Helen was a qualified teacher educated at the University of Hull. David had his calling to ministry in the Anglican Church, and he could have had any choice of parish. He chose the parish that was poor and one encumbered with an old church.

St Paul's Church was built in 1856 and consecrated in that year by the first bishop of Manchester. During its first hundred years, in a district that experienced grinding poverty, it suffered the ill effects of inadequate funding for maintenance and the consequence of dire atmospheric pollution. In 1968, David Wyatt arrived as the parish priest. He contacted Stephen Dykes Bower, surveyor to Westminster Abbey. Together, they put in hand an extensive programme of repair and adornment. The church, the parish rooms, the garden wall and gates were listed in 2003.

David and Helen Wyatt never left Salford. The people in need have changed. Today, it is the recent immigrants from Africa and Asia. In spite of their age, they still work tirelessly to help the many needy people who come to their door.

It was summer of 1976. It was hot. There was a heatwave on. It was the hottest summer since records began. Abba's hit song "Dancing Queen" was playing on the radio. There was also a drought, and water restrictions were in place. Harold Wilson had resigned earlier in the year as PM, and James Callahan was the new Labour PM. Margret Thatcher was the leader of the opposition, the first woman in Britain to ever lead a major political party.

I had received the results of the second-year examinations. I had failed a couple of subjects in my second year at university. As these were core subjects, the university asked me to repeat the year. The three-year course had suddenly become four. I was extremely disappointed with myself and in a low, depressed state.

Overseas phone calls were very expensive. The only communication with my parents who were in Africa was through letters. The Wyatts had by default become my parents in England. Like any parents, they also played a big part in keeping me motivated through my university course. I had to break the news to my father. He had struggled to send me to England. He had taken early retirement from the government service in Sri Lanka and gone to Africa. He was based in Malawi where he had been appointed the head of the telecommunication service there. I vividly remember making that call from a phone box with many coins ready to keep feeding the meter. It was an emotional call. My father was supportive; he assured me it was OK. He would pay the fees for another year, and he wanted me to continue.

But I was not happy. I seriously considered giving it up. The economy was picking up. I was not restricted from working as I was a British citizen. I could get a job, get on with life. It was Helen who counselled me. She used every occasion to keep talking to me, never making it seem like she was intruding, but she sensed what I was going through and knew I was considering packing it in.

The fact that I continued and completed my degree at Salford, I have to give a lot of credit for that to Helen Wyatt.

Meeting people outside the university helped me. Being part of the community and the people who visited the church meant I got to know more local people. I had a life outside of the university. I took a job as a bar waiter in the Salford Rugby League Club.

Soccer, or football as it was known in England, was and still is the most popular sport in the country. Even during the recession of the '70s, loyal fans would rather starve or miss a few pints of beer than give up their Saturday afternoon at the game. Salford was the adjoining suburb to Old Trafford, the home of Manchester United football club. David Wyatt was a fan. Other local young men in the community who I was acquainted with and were my age were also fans. Although I was not a fan of soccer, I followed and got interested in the game. You inevitably were swept in the enthusiasm if you lived in England. I went to a few matches to watch Man U play at Old Trafford.

While football was universal in England, rugby league had developed into a sport for the working class and was most popular in the northern part of Britain. The big clubs were concentrated in Lancashire and Yorkshire. Salford had its own rugby league club. Some of the others being in Wigan, Leeds, and St. Helens.

The Salford rugby league club had a variety club called the Willows as part of its complex in Weaste, Salford. It was part of an effort by the then-chairman, Brian Snape, to bring couples to the game. Salford had a winning formula under Snape. The Friday night and Sunday matches would draw crowds of 7,000 when other rugby league clubs would be happy with 2,000. They had won the championship in 1975.

The Willows would have shows on a Thursday and on weekends where touring entertainers and comedians would be headlined with local acts supporting to make up a full evening of entertainment. The Willows was a sit-down venue, with dinner served while you were entertained. It could hold up to about 640 people. I answered an advertisement in the *Manchester Evening News* for "drinks waiters" at the club and got selected. I had applied for many jobs, and the unemployment situation was such that you had to visit the premises, show up, and beg for the job.

The customers at the Willows were mainly working-class people who were extremely generous tippers. They drank a lot. As a drinks waiter, we were given a cash float at the beginning of the evening. We would take the order from tables, pay for the drinks from the bar, and then have to collect the money from customers. That was the hard part. Some customers refused to pay. At the end of the night, we had to reconcile the float. What you had left were the tips. It was crowded and very noisy. There were many customers who would make their own way to the bar to order their drinks. We had to fight for the attention of the person behind the bar. I had to develop, over time, a relationship with all the staff behind the bar so they served me as soon as I approached the bar with an order. I quickly worked out that the more orders I took and delivered to the table, my tips would be bigger at the end of the night. The basic wages were minimal; you relied on tips for your income.

Each waiter was assigned a number of tables. Some tables did not tip. I took the order, delivered the drinks, and was given the exact amount for the drinks. No tip. Effort wasted, get back to the next order. I was the only Asian waiter and an easy target for racial comments. I took it on the chin. It was uncomfortable, but it made me stronger. Some comedians on stage would target you, while working, in their routine; you learned to keep a low profile. After the event, we had to help clean up, prepare the place for the next day, collect all the glasses, and help with the washing up. After work, late in the night, I had to walk on the narrow, cobbled streets back to the St. Paul's Rectory. I had cash on me as I carried home my tips. The pubs were closing up at the same time, and there were many drunks on the streets. It was cold and windy on many nights. "F—— Paki!" was the shout many times. I had my tips hidden in my shoes. I was sober, never drank at work. I was happy to make some decent pocket money. I quietly avoided confrontation and made my way home.

During the university holidays, I would take to hiking alone in the Lake District and the other places in England. I would plan my trip meticulously—walk in the day and rest at hostels of the Youth Hostel Association (YHA) at night. I would have the bookings done at the various hostels and calculate the time and distance to get from one hostel to the other. I would equip myself with detailed maps, carry my rucksack, and walk. I learnt the difference between being alone and lonely. I learnt that being alone is a natural state for humans. I learnt during this period how to be comfortable with myself. They say it's important to know yourself before you get to know others. Unless you reach this state of knowing yourself, it's hard to aspire to lead others.

I made several trips to London from Salford. It was a four- or five-hour journey by coach. London was attractive as it was livelier. I had many of my friends from Sri Lanka studying there and a few of my relatives living in London. It was a required dose of nostalgia for me, enjoying the food, the company, and the relaxed banter one can only have when you are in the company of friends and relatives who have watched you grow. I needed that too badly from time to time. It's all these experiences that keep you grounded and provide a reality check. Every trip inspired me; it was the fuel I needed to keep going, in Salford.

I repeated the second year and found some new friends. My original batch colleagues were passing out that year. It took a lot to be motivated and keep going. I passed my exams and entered the final year.

I completed my final exams in May of 1978. I had passed with my bachelors of science in electronic communications. Not many understood what telecommunications was. It had not had its moment and its impact yet. We still had computers in the university that occupied a whole floor of the building. Access was strictly limited. One had to punch in cards to program the computer in the FORTRAN language. You were given a slot in time for the use of the computer.

In 1978, Bill Gates, also my age, twenty-three, had dropped out of college at eighteen and formed a company called Microsoft. In that year, they had eleven employees and had completed their first million dollars in sales. They decided that year to shift this young company to Seattle. That year, Bell Labs launched a trial of the first commercial cellular network in Chicago using Advanced Mobile Phone System (AMPS), an analogue, first-generation mobile technology. Martin Cooper, the father of the mobile phone, was still working at Motorola. He had invented the first phone in 1973 and had continuously refined and reduced the size. In 1978, it was still the size of a large brick.

The ARPANET experiment formally completed that year. This was a forerunner to the free and open Internet.

I did not know it then, but I had graduated at the time the foundations were being laid for the three biggest transformation in our lives—the personal computer, the mobile phone, and the Internet.

At the age of twenty-three, I was still not sure what I really wanted to do. I could not see a very bright future in telecommunications.

The jobs on offer were working for the three major vendors in England at that time—Plessey, STC, or GEC. The other option was to join the post office telecommunications department.

During the year, we had what was called the "milk round." Companies would visit the university and provide information about the company and their products and the graduate jobs that were available. Unemployment was still high in the UK, and the number of graduates looking for positions was more than the jobs available. Most of the jobs available were for research and development positions. I knew that I did not want a desk job. The only other option was to take a field job. There were limited opportunities for graduates in field jobs. They preferred diploma or apprentice candidates with hands-on experience.

GEC Telecommunications offered me a field job as a commissioning engineer; I decided to accept that offer. The company was based in Coventry, had its factory and its offices there. GEC's main customer was the British post office telecommunications. After some initial training in Coventry, I was ready for work. The routine was that I was posted to a customer's site somewhere in England, Wales, or Scotland. Initially working with a senior engineer, I would have to live in a bed-and-breakfast place during the week and return home for the weekends. I continued to keep my base at the Wyatts in Salford and would travel back there for the weekends.

I loved the job. The main form of transmission of signals across the country was still by coaxial cables. Optical fibre was still in the research labs. GEC supplied, installed, and commissioned these cable systems for the British post office. Every few kilometres, the cables signals had to be amplified and passed along. These cable systems were laid along the roads from one telephone exchange to the other. We were given a Ford Transit van. In the back would be traffic cones, flashing lights to indicate men at work, and test equipment. The first part of the job was to locate the manhole by the side of the road or by some field. All we had was a description and address. We would stop the van and sometimes spend time walking up and down the road to locate the manhole. There were usually two of us working on the job. Once we found it, we would have to lift the heavy concrete covers off. We would then release the air pressure of the sealed box that contained the amplifiers. The air pressure was needed to keep the box watertight. Once we finished, we had to reseal the box and pump the box with air to seal it back again. We had to observe there was no leak of air.

My love of the job was not because I had to be outside in the cold and snow on the side of the road, opening a manhole, stepping inside, and taking measurements on this cable system. It was not because I had to stay in some cramped bed with a shared toilet in a bed-and-breakfast guest house. It was not because I was the junior and was given all the worst jobs to do.

I loved the job because of the freedom. I had no bosses looking over me in an office. My office was the Ford Transit van. Paperwork was done in the BPO telephone exchange. I took instructions and reported back on the fixed phone only when I had access to one. There were no mobiles. I broadly knew my tasks, and the rest was up to me, how I executed it. They were interested in the results, not the how and when. I loved this freedom. Granted, I loved the summers, travelling around the most beautiful English countryside, down in Cornwall, up in Wales, the Yorkshire moors. I loved that the only place to have lunch was the quaintest pubs on the way to somewhere. There was always a pub. Meticulous planning would go into our day to make sure we were passing the best pub on the route. I really loved the job.

I could have continued in this job forever. There were many who were my seniors who would not exchange this freedom for anything.

The pay was also good. You got a daily allowance to cover all the food and bed-and-breakfast costs. Usually, we found we could live on the daily allowance, and we did not touch our monthly salary. I was saving good money. I learnt fast and was given bigger responsibilities. I would call the head office in Coventry a few weeks before I finished my assignment and inquired on the new assignments coming up.

It was on one such call they told me they were looking for engineers to go to Nigeria.

Chapter 4

Into Africa

Nigeria was under military rule in 1979 when I arrived. The country had gone through many military coups since its independence in 1960.

In 1967, Col. Ojukwu had announced the cessation of the southeast of Nigeria from the rest of the country. Southeast Nigeria was home mainly of the Igbo (pronounced *eebo*) tribe. The Igbo people are mainly Christian. They converted and became Christian during the colonial rule of Britain. Because of the Atlantic slave trade from this part of the continent, many current African Americans are of Igbo decent.

The other major tribes of Nigeria were the Hausa, who were mainly in the north of the country, and the Yoruba, who were from the south-west of the country. These three tribes made up more than 70 percent of the population. The politics and the political parties were divided along tribal lines. This led to dissent and animosity as one tribe gained power over the other.

Col Ojukwu announced the creation of the Republic of Biafra.

The mainly Muslim Hausa tribe were opposed to this move, and the Biafra civil war ensued for three years. A bitter and brutal civil war resulted in a million civilian casualties, mainly from famine and fighting. The country was blockaded by the Nigerian army as part of the strategy to win the war, and many people starved to death.

The country, although sitting on vast reserves of oil, had not at that time fully exploited its natural wealth. It suffered years of negative growth. There was yellow fever. It was a prerequisite to have the vaccination before you travelled to the country.

GEC Telecommunications had won a major contract to supply equipment to the government-run telecommunications company. This was part of a much larger project to bring basic communications to all parts of Nigeria. The company had established itself in many of the major cities of Nigeria. I was posted to the south-east part of the country and went to Enugu, the capital of Anambra State. This was the part of the country that had wanted to be Biafra. It had suffered most in the civil war. Bitter divisions remained in the country, and the atrocities of the Biafra war were not forgotten in this part of the country. In 1979 when I arrived, it was only nine years since the cessation of hostilities.

I was twenty-four, hardly a year since graduation, and I was an expatriate. Little did I know then that this pattern of being an expat, working away from my home, would continue through my career, in Djibouti, Mauritania, South Yemen, Bangladesh, India, Sri Lanka, and Malaysia.

In Nigeria, I witnessed extreme poverty for the first time in my life. I also witnessed horrific violence. Under military rule, the army was present everywhere. They would beat up people on the street.

The company had rented a large house in Enugu. It was located in one of the better suburbs of Enugu. It was fully furnished, fully air-conditioned, and with generators for back up, as the power situation in the country was really bad. There were frequent, unscheduled power cuts. In the heat of Nigeria, if you did not have relief from either a fan or AC, it was unbearable. The company had hired cooks and cleaners and provided this "home" environment for the young bachelors from England.

The office and warehouse was a few kilometres away. We were all given Land Rovers to drive.

The Enugu house was well managed. The manager in charge of the Enugu office was Paul Fonseka. He was mixed Sri Lankan and English, fair in complexion, and could pass for being Spanish. There was a mix of people in the team. Paul ran a good operation and made sure the standards and discipline were maintained in the house.

This was not easy among the bunch of young English bachelors who loved their beer and fun. I admired Paul and how he handled the team. He had quite a responsibility, making sure the team were safe in this hostile environment. He also instilled discipline in the house. There were rules. Meal times were fixed. You had to be there during that time for meals or get something outside yourself. The meals were served by the staff all dressed in white, first course, usually a soup, followed by the second and third course. The Enugu house was a safe haven, and I would welcome the times I would return there after my assignments in the bush.

Each assignment in the bush lasted three to five weeks. By the end of that time, you were just longing for some conversation, a proper meal, reading the papers, and having a few beers at the "snake pit." That's what we called the local nightclub. They called it the snake pit as the girls would hiss at you to attract your attention. The night club had fantastic live music with the unique West African rhythms and beats.

The main project had started many years before. The objective of the project was to bring basic telephone service to the major and smaller towns in Anambra State. The cabling around the towns to the residences and offices had been done, the telephone exchange was being completed, and GEC provided the link or the transmission from the town to the capital Enugu so that long distance calls from that town could be connected to the rest of the country and the world.

The first team on site from GEC would be the installers. The installers were older guys who had been at this game for a long time. They loved this lifestyle, living as expats. They saved a lot of money, paid no tax, and most of them owned many properties back home in the UK. There were no hotels or guest houses one could stay at in the remote parts of the country. GEC owned a few caravans. These were self-contained and towable. Each could comfortably accommodate two persons. It had a private bedroom, an attached bath, and kitchen. They were air-conditioned and comfortable. They were quite large, and the installers would be the ones who would latch this to the back of their Land Rovers and tow it to the site.

The site was the compound belonging to the Nigerian Post and Telecommunications (NPT) and would have a building where our equipment was housed. There would be a large, forty-metre or sixty-metre steel tower in the yard. The tower was used to mount the microwave links to carry the signals to the next site.

The installers would connect the power to the caravan and would have done all the groundwork on this site. They would have found out how you get water, where the best place to buy food, and who to trust. Once the installation was complete, they would hand over to me as the commissioning engineer, and I would take over the caravan. They would move on to the next job. The caravan was my home till I finished the assignment. Each assignment would take from three to five weeks.

The first few days would be a handover, and we would both sleep in the same caravan, as it could comfortably sleep two, and I would get to know the ropes. Water was a major problem. Each day the caravan tank had to be filled. The water was available at certain times of the day. We always had a man Friday with us who would clean the caravan and also cook. His job was to make sure the water tank was filled so we could take a shower. The toilet was chemical. Once the handover was done, the installer would leave. I was on my own, like Robinson Crusoe and his man Friday.

I was young and inexperienced. I had been working for just a year. In the UK, you had great support back at head office, and usually a technical fault was easily diagnosed with a few calls back to the office or the labs. Spare parts could be delivered overnight. The reality here was that you were on your own. There was no back up, and I was thrown in the deep end without a life jacket.

Prior to my assignment to Nigeria, I had hardly any experience of commissioning microwave radio systems. In university, I had done communication theory. I had not done any practical work. Most if not all the others in this job were not degreed engineers but technical diploma holders who had hands-on, practical training. I learnt fast. I had to.

The only form of communication with the office in Enugu was an HF radio. It was one of the first things the installers set up. The antenna was a long wire one would string up one of the legs of the tower. You had to press to talk—"Enugu, Enugu, this is Vijay calling. Do you read?"—hoping there would be a response. Sometimes it was so gargled you could hardly make out what was being said. Paul's reassuring voice was mostly at the other end. He was genuinely concerned and kept track of the progress of the project from his office in Enugu.

My only connection to the outside world was a transistor radio. I listened to the BBC news regularly. There were no telephones; we were bringing communications for the first time to that town. There were no computers; there was no e-mail. Bill Gates and Microsoft had only thirteen employees, and they were still working with the BASIC computer language. The Internet was not thought of. Seven universities in the USA were just meeting to see how they could connect their mainframes to talk to each other.

I was on my own. If I had a problem, I had to work it out myself.

GEC made multiplex equipment, and I was familiar with this kit. Multiplex equipment combined several individual voice channels to one. It was like having several pipes of water combined to one pipe. This was then further combined again so that the one pipe containing all the voice channels could be transmitted over the microwave radio to the next place. Here it was separated again into individual voice channels. We were using a US-manufactured radio system from Granger. We were all new to this technology. Gradually, as I did more and more sites, I got familiar with the Granger microwave systems, and I gained confidence. Before each new assignment, before I left Enugu, I would stock up with spares as I got to know the rogue units that usually failed and made my life miserable.

The NPT site compound was fenced, and there was a guard at the gate. I would not venture out of that gate. It was dirty and crowded outside, and there was not much there for me to see. Not many in the village spoke English. It was just work and my caravan. That was my life for the duration of the assignment. Work could start as early as I wanted, and I would keep at it, working till late, till I was exhausted. There was no TV. The best you could do was read old newspapers and magazines from the UK. I kept working till late, testing and sorting out the good equipment from the faulty.

Quality was not an essential part of the UK manufacturing culture. Many units were faulty on arrival. It was good to sort this out early, see what you had that was working and what was not. I would then spend time trying to repair the faulty cards and get them working. The longer I took, the longer I was stuck alone here, on site. If spares or components to fix the faulty unit were needed, I had to radio Enugu and get them to send it over by some transport. Usually, this meant waiting for one of the other engineers or installers to be travelling past your site. I was thoroughly engrossed in my work.

This was not digital equipment. This was analogue technology where you had to tweak many different parts to get a decent signal. Sometimes you tweak one component to its optimum and another component degrades in performance. You need to keep going back and forth till you got both components working optimally. Success meant the links all working end to end and calls being made from the remote town I was working in to Enugu. We also had to prove that the calls could get beyond Enugu to the capital, Lagos.

They usually had a formal opening of the telephone exchange with tribal dancers, the politicians and ministers coming over to take the glory for the new service that connected the town to the rest of the country. Since my job was the last link, there was a lot of pressure for me to finish the work and for them to do the exchange cutover in time. Many times, I was not ready. I fixed the situation so that the connection was hard-wired to Enugu. All were happy that the ceremonial call was able to be made. I continued to work till the job was properly done.

One particular day, I had trouble with the next station on the link, which was about 30 Km away. I was testing the microwave link all the way back to Enugu. I figured out that it was a possible problem in the next relay site. I usually don't drive alone; I take my man Friday with me. This time I decided to risk it.

He was cooking my dinner. The road was fairly isolated. I jumped into the Land Rover with some test equipment and drove to the site. I was confronted on this journey with a scene that left a scar for life.

A man had been probably knocked down by a vehicle; he was clearly dead and lying on the road. There were no other persons around. That scene was bad enough and disturbing. Vultures had gathered around the body and were picking on the body of the man. Vultures tend to attack a carcass from any orifice they can find. This particular vulture from the group had its head up the rectum and was pulling out the entrails of this human. Much as I wanted to turn away, I couldn't. It was horrific. *Should I stop? What should I do? What could I do?*

I was confused, helpless, and traumatised. I just kept driving on. It was dangerous to stop. I could not speak the language, and an expat in a Land Rover was an easy kidnap target. I drove quickly to the site. Once I got there, I called and got one of the workers in the exchange to go get my man Friday from the Caravan. I asked him to get on a bus and come to the site. I needed someone to be with me on my way back. I will never forget that day or that image.

I was alone. At night, the darkness would be absolute. There was limited electricity in these towns. I probably had one of the few connections. The generators would purr through the night, keeping the telephone exchange and my caravan with power. At night, quite often I would sit on a folding chair outside the caravan and gaze at this fantastic display of stars, a display you will only see in a dark, remote place. There was no one to talk to. The man Friday hardly spoke English; he talked in pigeon English that I had to get used to if I wanted to communicate. I was alone but not lonely. But being alone for such long periods, can send you crazy. There is only so much you can think about and so much you can read. I am sure this being alone, this isolation, affected me.

Despite this, I would go on, back to Enugu spend a few days, catch up with the gossip, have a few beers, load up the Land Rover, and out again to the next assignment. The money was good. For a young twenty-four-year-old, I was saving quite a bit, enough on my return to England to put a deposit on a brand-new house in Northampton. But it was never about the money. There was something else driving me. I did not have a passion for engineering or for telecommunications, but I continued to enjoy this independence. I was my own boss. I loved that independence with a passion.

Due to the isolation and no communication, this independence was heightened in Nigeria compared to, say, working in England. But it was more than that. I knew in a small way I was also making a difference to those people in the towns of eastern Nigeria. These people who had suffered in the Biafra war, they were getting connected, getting telephone connections for the first time. I listened to some of the horrific things and the starvation that these people went through during the war. Here I was, doing something to improve their life. I was getting an inner satisfaction I could not have in England. I was making a difference.

There was a pool of man Fridays available at the office. We would be assigned one before we set out. My favourite man Friday was Raphael. He was short and always with a sad face. He would sit next to me in the Land Rover, and we would set out to the new assignment. Most of the other engineers and installers did not like him because he drank. He loved his palm wine, a local cheap brew, and he drank heavily. My job was to make sure he cooked and cleaned and filled water in the caravan before he hit the bottle. He had suffered badly in the Biafra War. He had lost his family through starvation. He had a lot to forget. I liked him because he was a good man. He was clean and had worked in an expat house before, so his cooking was good. He would spice up the food for me. He understood I would be upset if he drank before he had finished all his chores.

One day I asked Raphael to buy some chicken from the market for a stew. I was told by others who had him on other assignments that he was an expert at chicken stew. I was naive and thought he would go to the market and buy a few pieces of chicken for the stew. My place of work was in the building in the same compound as the caravan. It was forty metres to work, the shortest commute I have ever had in my life. I would often come back to the caravan for a cup of tea. One day, to my surprise, I found this live chicken tied to the steps of the caravan. I had not expected he would do the killing himself. Raphael wrung the chicken's neck, killing it, then skilfully plucked its feathers and cooked the chicken. It was the freshest chicken stew I had tasted, and I enjoyed it. He also killed one or two snakes prowling around the caravan. I do not know where they ended up. Having gone through this extended period of famine during the Biafra War, the Igbo ate anything that moved.

I never had the opportunity to go to church in Nigeria, and I missed the Sunday services at St. Paul's in Salford. But in the stillness of the night under the stars and alone, you connect spiritually in ways it is hard to put in words. I had not felt lonely; there was a sense of someone always being there.

I didn't have to take this assignment in Nigeria. I was quite comfortable in the UK. The choice was to wrench myself out of my comfort zone and try this role in Africa, a place I knew nothing about, a place where I had no one. The choice, though, made me grow more rapidly than I would have had I stayed in England. I matured faster as a man, I learnt more about myself and my capabilities, and I survived in a very hostile environment. There is no doubt in my mind that this stint in Nigeria prepared me for the later roles I undertook, prepared me for marriage, and changed a lot of my views on life.

It was December 1981. I was twenty-six. I had returned to England from Nigeria the year before. My stint in Nigeria had given me the means to put down a deposit and get on the housing ladder. I invested in a semidetached, brand-new house being built in Northampton. I bought this house off the plan. It had not been built as yet. I had endured being alone in Nigeria and had overcome many challenges. However, it had given me an economic leg up. The money I had saved by working in Nigeria was substantial for a young man, and I had saved enough to make a set of choices not available to my friends who had started working at the same time as I.

We are all fortunate that we live in a world where we have a choice of whom we marry. There are still parts of India and the subcontinent where they have child brides and arranged marriages where you find out who your partner is on the day of the wedding.

Today we have a simpler choice. Our choice now is if we get married or not. It's sad that more and more people are opting out of marriage or leaving it for later in their life. While there is no secret to the success of a marriage, it is a choice. It is a choice to sacrifice some personal freedom for a shared world that is bigger and more expansive than the singular world, a more expansive world in which the two can jointly grow and share the joys and the disappointments that are part of life together.

It's a choice that has risks. It's a choice many young people today are afraid to make because they have benefitted from a period of unprecedented economic growth in the world, so much so, that their lives are very comfortable. Marriage poses more of a threat to their way of life, their comfort zone that they don't see beyond the singular world. There is no right or wrong, but unless you challenge the complacency that will inevitably come with staying in your comfort zone, you will never know the person you ought to be. Marriage is supposed to shake you out of the comfort zone; it's a partnership, the only true and joined-at-the-hip sort of partnership most of us will make in life. In marriage, you share and get closer to someone who is a stranger. You start the marriage at ground zero. Every day you are together after that is a new experience, new challenges, adjustments, compromise. In marriage, you grow faster than you would grow if you were alone.

Some marriages don't work out. But to not get into marriage for fear that it might not work out is the wrong reason. Whether it works out or not, we get to know ourselves a little more in marriage.

The risks can be minimised but not eliminated if we marry when we are young. In early adulthood we are still flexible; we are not so set in our ways. We have not settled too much into a comfort zone.

Around the age of twenty-six, there must be some genetically triggered switch that goes into action.

I was enjoying my nomadic lifestyle and not ready to settle down and get married. Marriage was the furthest thing from my mind. So I am not sure why I purchased this asset, this house in Northampton.

I was working all over the country, travelling and living in bed-and-breakfast lodgings. My worldly possessions were all in Manchester at the Wyatts. I had my own room there, and I returned at weekends. Purchasing this house kind of forced me out of the nomadic lifestyle I was leading and let me put my first roots in England.

I left that December 1981 to Colombo to attend a wedding. I was to be best man at the wedding of my good friend, Yevindra. Yevi was studying for his degree in Manchester, and we had spent a lot of time together as students, and we got on really well. Yevi and I had gone to the same school, St. Thomas's College back in Sri Lanka, and we knew each other, but we would not be described as close friends in school.

In Manchester as struggling students, we got together very often, and our friendship grew to something special. Yevi worked as a waiter in an Indian restaurant, and I was a bar waiter at the Salford rugby club. Yevi turned out to be a really good cook, and we would often meet at Yevi's to consume a good rice and curry. I was particularly touched and honoured to be asked by Yevi to be best man at his wedding to Ymara, and I accepted.

It was on the morning after the wedding that I was confronted with this choice.

A family friend of Sharadha, who also was my relative, had suggested we meet. We were to meet at the Queen's Club tennis courts on a Sunday morning. Sharadha's sisters, Nirupa and Tina, were being coached in tennis, and she was going to be there with them. I went with a very open mind. I had no desire to settle down immediately, but I was not against marriage either. I had no idea what I was getting into. It was early morning. I had quite a lot to drink the previous night at the wedding. I had to be woken up. I was late for the meeting that had been arranged. The only form of transport available was a push bike. I had to be there in ten minutes. I was late. I peddled furiously.

I got there and used the back entrance and was able to observe Sharadha from behind the trees as I approached the tennis courts. She was reading a book. She was reading a book on the life of Idi Amin, the brutal dictator of Uganda. I learnt later she just picked the first book on her way out from home. I thought at the time it was strange she would be reading this rather serious book. We were introduced and exchanged small chat. This was a door, one where you have no idea what's on the other side. Both of us were confronted with this choice. There would have been no repercussions either to me or to her if we decided not to pursue this choice. We were still young. Sharadha was twenty-three.

Over the next few days, we met a few times, alone, still strangers, making small talk. I am not the best conversationalist, and Sharadha found it hard. She labelled me a quiet one. We did have a lot in common. We were both the eldest in our families. Our families were of very similar backgrounds. Both of us had been to England for our tertiary education and had managed on our own. We had tasted the independence of being alone.

As with any choice of this magnitude, it was a choice with risks. High risks give even higher returns. Would the risks be less if I had known Sharadha for a much longer time before I made a commitment to get married? Since I can write now with hindsight after thirty-two years of marriage, I contend that it really would not have mattered. You really don't get to know a person till you have made that full and final commitment of marriage.

However long you have been dating a person, the day after the honeymoon, it's ground zero.

In marriage the family too play an important part of defining the culture of that union. Having in-laws who do not judge but accept the differences in their new sons or daughters makes a big difference to any marriage. I was fortunate to be welcomed into the family of Albert and Ranji.

You have to go into marriage assuming failing is impossible. The relationship needs to be built brick by brick. It's a partnership. Each one will have a role in the partnership, and there cannot be a conflict in these roles. Each one needs his or her space within the marriage, and yet each one needs to have a commitment to make it work.

We both returned to England after meeting on that day and continued our courtship and getting to know each other, planning the wedding. On the fourth of September 1982, we returned to Sri Lanka and got married at the All Saints Church in Borella.

Chapter 5

My Roots

I am quite fortunate that I can trace one couple in history who begat both my father's side of the family and my mother's side of the family. My family tree does not spread out in a fan; it converges to this particular person and his wife. I have a common ancestor on the paternal and maternal side.

I am also fortunate that my grandfather on my mother's side had taken the trouble to research and document the family history. His book, *The House of Nevins*, starts with information about the father of my common ancestor. His name was Muttucumarar, and he lived from 1770 to 1840. Essentially the recorded story of our family starts in 1770.

In 1770, the island of Ceylon was under the rule of the Dutch. The Dutch had first landed in Zeylan, as they called it, in 1602. They first landed in the coastal town of Batticaloa on the east coast of the Island. Parts of the country were then under Portuguese rule. The Dutch East India Company, also called VOC, was a joint-stock company that controlled the trade between Asia and Europe. They were based in Batavia on the island of Java. Batavia is now Jakarta, the capital of Indonesia.

The Dutch were frequent visitors to Ceylon and had talks with the king of Kandy about allied action against the Portuguese. A Dutch/Portuguese war and some misunderstanding with the king led the Dutch to decide to conquer the island.

The Dutch began their rule of the island in 1640. They were unable to conquer the interior because they were more concerned with the threat to their seaborne empire from the English and the French. They left the Kandy kings their kingdom in the centre of the Island and kept control of the coast. They divided the area they ruled into three provinces. The governor was based in Colombo, and commanders administered the other two in Jaffna and Galle.

1770, it was the year that Captain Cook discovered Australia.

In Jaffna, the Dutch encouraged small holders to grow tobacco and other vegetables. They encouraged them to grow palmyra products, onions, gourds, chillies, turmeric, and ginger. The VOC imported rice into Jaffna. They made money on the import of rice and the export of the tobacco and vegetables. The small holders, too, thrived with the trade and made as much money as the VOC. It was hard work, as the soil and arid conditions of the Jaffna Peninsula were not naturally conducive to agriculture.

During the Dutch reign, our ancestors were Orthodox Hindus. The family lived in the village of Maviddapuram in the north of Ceylon. Muttucumara's father was a trustee of the temple in the village. Muttucumar married and moved to another village called Sanguvelly. He had four daughters. Longing for a son, he made a pilgrimage to the Sithamparam Temple in South India to make a vow so he could have a son. His wish was fulfilled. His fifth child was my great-great-grandfather, William Nevins Sithamparampillai.

Sithamparampillai means child of Sithamparam in Tamil, the name of the temple where the vow was made. William Nevins was my common ancestor. However, that was not his name at birth.

Hindu custom called for the father's name to be first followed by your own name. So William Nevins was named as Muttucumarar Sithamparampillai when he was born in 1820.

In 1815, the Dutch were conquered by Napoleonic France. Their leaders became refugees in London. No longer able to govern their part of the island effectively, the Dutch transferred the rule of Ceylon to the British.

Two years earlier, in 1813 the American missionaries had arrived in Ceylon. As this was just after the Anglo-American war in 1812, the British were extremely suspicious of the Americans. The Americans landed in Galle and then travelled to Jaffna. The British colonial office in Ceylon restricted the Americans to the relatively small Jaffna Peninsula. The British were not keen on them having access to the rest of the Island.

Missionaries from the Methodist mission in England were all over the rest of the Island. The Americans did a much better job of educating the Hindu Tamil in the north than the British did in educating the Sinhalese in the south. This led to an imbalance in the education of the two communities. The seed of division was planted. This seed grew over time and led to a civil war 200 years later. It's ironic that the War of 1812 between Britain and USA would affect this tiny Island in such a way.

The Americans missionaries built churches and schools in the Jaffna Peninsula. They were funded by the churches in New England in the USA. They also made efforts to provide collegiate-level education by founding the Batticotta Seminary in 1823. Jaffna College in Vaddukodai is now on the former seminary site.

It is likely that William Nevins was a bright boy and that he was tutored and coached in Tamil and Sanskrit, another ancient language. He was selected at the age of twelve to enter the American Wesleyan Missionary Seminary at Batticotta.

The seminary had only about 170 places, and each year only twenty to thirty students were selected. The missionaries were very selective. There were many applicants for the few positions available, and it would have been Sithamparampillai's father who would have played a major role in pushing his young son to try his luck. It's likely that the father wanted his son to get the best of education available at that time. It is likely the father believed his son would take all the advantages of the opportunity in education the seminary offered but return home a Hindu. In fact, many students did just that. There was no compulsion to convert. However, all students were closely monitored, and in archive reports from the seminary to the US, it can be seen that each student was given a rating to indicate if they were likely to convert or remain "heathen."

Every child entering the seminary had to leave all vestiges of their Hindu culture, including his name before being accepted at the seminary. All the students were given English names, and they had to use these English names throughout the times they were in the seminary, which could be eight years. The seminary was a boarding school, and so the students lived there for the duration of the studies. This was to give them the maximum exposure to the Christian education, manners, and culture, with the hope they would convert. William Nevins was the names he was given at the seminary.

Muttucumarar Sithamparampillai became William Nevins Sithamparampillai.

The American missionary's prime objective was to win converts in Ceylon, a country with two strong entrenched religions of Hindus in the north and Buddhists in the south. A secondary objective was the founding of schools. The missionaries found after much trial and error that it was not easy to convert these heathens. The only interest the locals had was in the Western education they could provide. The missionaries found that providing an education was their best chance of exposing young boys and girls to Christianity. The intention was that some children might convert. From the parents' and students' points of view, this was a passport to prosperity, an English education.

The American missionaries did not insist on the renunciation of idolatry. They also did not insist on any formal declaration of Christian belief. There were none of these preconditions put before admission to the seminary.

However, they did insist on a few things. Each student, including young William Nevins, was required to attend morning prayer and evening devotions and to attend services on Sunday at the chapel. No applying of the Hindu ashes on the forehead was allowed, and participation in Hindu religious observances or worship, even when you went home, was a disciplined offence.

These were well-understood conditions of their admission. All the students and their parents voluntarily complied in order to participate in all the advantages that this education would provide. The seminary kept records of the students and filed reports back to the United States. The missions were funded by the churches and congregations in the United States. All students had English names, and apart from their scholarly abilities, they reported if the student had shown interest in becoming a Christian or was converted or not interested. Hindus were referred as heathens.

When William Nevins Sithamparampillai graduated from the seminary, he was a Christian. It is likely that during his time at the seminary he made a choice. He made a choice to leave the religion of his family, a choice made that would affect his children, grandchildren, and generations after that.

He returned to the seminary as a teacher until it closed in 1855. William Nevins devoted his life to educating others. He was headmaster of the Wesleyan Missionary School, which later became Jaffna Central College. He also founded a school that was later to become Jaffna Hindu College. He died in 1889.

Due to the choices made by both William Nevins and his father, we changed from being Hindus to being educated and Christian.

William Nevins and his wife Margret were my common ancestor.

My mother's side came from one of William Nevins's sons. His name was Timothy Nevins. He followed his father into education and was teacher and principal of Jaffna Hindu College and was the principal of Trinity College in Kandy.

My father's side came from one of William Nevins's daughters. Rasamma who married Vallipuram Watson.

The family name Watson also was a result of the conversion of an ancestor from Hindu to Christianity.

One of the pioneer converts when the American missionaries arrived was a Hindu *poosari*, which is the term for the person who assists in the Hindu temple. There is no record of his name before he converted. On conversion, he took the name of Rev. Richard Watson.

Rev. Richard Watson was an enthusiastic missionary and converted many in his own family who then each subsequently took the name of Watson. The Christian name clearly differentiated them from their Hindu relatives and brethren.

Rev. Richard Watson's nephew (his sister's son), whose original name was Vallipuram, took the name of Vallipuram Watson when he was converted by his uncle. Thus, the name of Watson became our family name.

I was curious how and why the name Watson was chosen by the Hindu poosari. When he took the name of Rev. Richard Watson, was it the name of the missionary who converted him? This was common.

We are not sure if there was indeed an American missionary by the name of Rev. Richard Watson. However, at about this time, there was a Rev. Richard Watson in England who was very influential in the Wesleyan Methodist movement in England. He had a pivotal role in raising funds and reporting on the progress of missionaries to Ceylon and other parts of the world at that time. He was the secretary to the Wesleyan Methodist Missionary Society in England. He never travelled to Ceylon, but he was instrumental in choosing the missionaries and also funding their missions and reporting their progress to the wider audience in England. He wrote letters to the missions, and his sermons were published and sent to the various missions. His name would have been prominent in any Wesleyan newsletters and publications. He also played a role in the abolishment of slavery later in life. There are a few books about his life and the letters he wrote. It is entirely possible that the Hindu poosari on conversion to Christianity took the name of this prominent leader of the Wesleyan Methodist movement as his new Christian name.

The letters of the Rev. Richard Watson in England, on the conversion of a priest in Ceylon, gives an insight how important a convert this Hindu Poosari would have been to the American Missionaries.

> I congratulate you on the last news from Ceylon [he writes to Jabez Bunting, then in Leeds]. God seems

very evidently to own that mission. A circumstance so encouraging as the conversion of the priest Sikarras has not, to the best of my recollection, occurred at so early a period in the experience of any other mission to the east. On all sides, doors were opening on smooth hinges. Missionaries were beginning to send home formidable weapons which savages had abandoned for the tools of civilization, grotesque and horrible idols as specimens of those that were being festooned with cobwebs or left to the company of bats.

Memoirs of the Life and Writings of the Rev. Richard Watson, published in 1834.

The Hindu poosari, given his status in the Hindu Community may have wanted to take the name of a prominent leader of the missionaries as his new name. Rev. Richard Watson letters and writings to the missions abroad would have been available to everyone and his name known among the American Wesleyan missionaries in Jaffna. I have no documented evidence. It's a theory that this Hindu poosari took the name of this prominent English missionary leader, and so the name Watson came to being in our family.

I was fortunate to be born into this family of educational luminaries. They had used their own privileged position being educated by the American missionaries to educate others in the community.

We have no choice into which family we are born; much like the servants who had no choice as to how many talents they got in the parable in the Bible. It is my favourite parable.

The parable is recorded by both Matthew and Luke in the Bible. The parable goes like this.

A wealthy landlord is about to go off on a long journey. In one version he has to leave in a bit of a hurry and is not sure he would return. Before he leaves, he calls his three servants and entrusts them with his liquid assets or cash. To one servant he gives five talents. A talent is about fifteen years of wages of a labourer, a significant amount of money.

To another servant he gives two talents and to a third servant he gives one talent. He gives this to each servant according to their ability. He then went away.

The first servant who was given five talents traded with the money and doubled the money. So did the second servant, he doubled his money too. The third hid his master's money by digging a hole in the ground, kind of "hid it under the mattress."

When the wealthy landlord returned, he called his servants to give an account of the money he had entrusted them with. The first mentions that he has doubled the money. The landlord is really pleased and says he will be given much more responsibility and that he would enter into the joy of his master. The second was also given the same response.

The third servant when asked responded by saying that, knowing the master was a hard man, reaping where he did not sow and gathering where he did not winnow, he was afraid, and so he hid the money in the ground. He offered the master the same money that was given to him.

The landlord was furious with him. "You wicked and slothful servant! You knew that I reap where I have not sowed and gather where I have not winnowed? Then you ought to have invested my money with the bankers, and at my coming I should have received what was my own with interest." So he took the talent from him and gives it the one who had ten talents. "For to everyone who has, will be more given, and he will have abundance; but from him who has not, even what he has will be taken away."

To me, this is a parable about life.

We have no choice into which family we are born, much like the servants who had no choice as to how many talents they got. But we have complete freedom and the choice to make what we want of the situation we are in, the family we are born into, to then double or triple the return. The master did not leave specific or detailed instructions to the servants on how they should behave with the talents they were given.

"Our talents are the gift that God gives to us. What we make of our talents is our gift back to God."—Leo Buscaglia.

Some are born into a poor family, others into a rich family, but everyone born into some family. We don't have a choice about the family we are born into. But we do have a choice of what we do once we are in that family. It is not always about the wealth of the family that determines your success. To accept that notion is to give up on life. It was after all the grandson of a poor Kenyan goat farmer who became the president of the most powerful nation in the world.

Today, when a manager goes on leave, he is often rushed, trying hard to get as much done so that things run smoothly during his absence. Very often he would assign tasks to his direct reports. He would assign the tasks according to their ability. Decision-making will also be delegated to each, depending on his or her ability. When he returns from leave, he will find that some have used the opportunity, taken the initiative and made decisions in his absence, and moved the workload along, perhaps even doubling production. They would have taken some risk. There will always be one, though, who fearing the manager's wrath has procrastinated on some decision and left the matter pending for his return. He did not want to take ownership or responsibility preferring to wait for the manager's return. Playing safe also has a consequence.

The parable is about growth and choosing growth over doing nothing. There is nothing predetermined in our life. To lie back and expect that things will come to pass is the choice of the third servant. We have to take the initiative. There is no compulsion to make a choice for change.

Many of the choices presented to us have risks. But regardless, your growth is guaranteed. If you fail, you grow. If you succeed, you grow. You won't grow unless you plunge yourself into life and grab the opportunities presented to you.

In 2009, we were living and working in Kolkata, India. As I sit in the back of the Innova, driven to work every morning, I am comfortable in my air-conditioned car. You can't help but get drawn to observe these families living on the street. They are the poorest people you would find anywhere in the world. They are worse off than the slum dwellers; at least slum dwellers have some form of a roof over their head. I see the kids playing. I see them defecating openly on the street. It's their home, and they have no thought about it being shameful, that the world passing them by can see them using the street as their toilet. They are happy. The older kids, even at the age of six or seven, will be taking care of the babies like an adult. They cook their food in open fires on the street. The municipality dumps all the household garbage at a certain point, and they sort it out— separating the plastic, the glass, whatever can be recycled—and by selling these recycled items they make a meagre living. It is a smelly, awful job.

I sometimes wonder how it would be if I were born into one of these families. I have to conclude that I would be just like them. Whatever feelings I currently have, the feeling of shame of sitting on the edge of the pavement exposing my bottom to the traffic and defecating, I only have because of the family I was born into. I too would just be happy as those children, because I would not know any different.

It would be the only way for me to survive. I would be more interested in my basic needs. *Where was my next meal coming from?*

The trip every morning was a blessing for me. It continually reminded me and made me appreciate what I have.

And yet these are God's children. They make their living sorting this rubbish, and they take risks. They can move out of their comfort zones and try to do better. Some children get an opportunity through an NGO to get a basic education. Many NGOs struggle to get the parents to let their children come to school as they are needed either to look after the rest of the family or to help in sorting this pile of rubbish, a vicious cycle—no labour no food. Yet like all parents, some understand how education can help their children to a better life, and they send them. These children then use this to further improve themselves and break from the abject poverty they were in.

It's much easier when you have one talent to double it than trying to double a much larger five talents.

I was born into a family that was equivalent to having a few talents. History will judge if I was like the first and second servant or the third.

Chapter 6

Home

We called England home for fifteen years. In 1989, we uprooted ourselves, sold our house, and moved to a new country.

After my return from Nigeria in 1980, I had continued to work with GEC in England. I continued working in the field, travelling the country, and living in bed-and-breakfast guest houses. I had seen the whole country up close, traversing not just the "A" roads but the smaller, quaint, secondary roads, villages, and numerous pubs. I loved the English countryside in summer. It was much harder in the winter, working outside in the cold and the rain.

After marriage, we settled in our house in Northampton.

The birth of the first child in a marriage will always be special. We welcomed our son Viruben in Northampton in early June.

Ranji my mother-in-law was with us during the time just before the birth and stayed on to show us the ropes. She had travelled from Sri Lanka to be with us, it was to be her eldest grandchild. It was such a blessing to have her there, her experience with her own seven children clearly obvious. Apart from bath time. That was painful to watch. She would pinch, squeeze, and vigorously rub the baby

Viruben, who was in shock. When it came to our turn we took a more gentle approach.

I had a special relationship with Ranji as a mother and friend. She peacefully passed away in her sleep in 2014.

At her memorial I delivered the eulogy and this was an extract:

> I was blessed that I could spend a short time with aunty Ranji the week before she journeyed on. She was tired, she had attended a party the night before where she had met all the old friends from Chilaw. She was tired but happy that she had met all the old friends. And yet after a few minutes she was up wanting to get something for me from the kitchen. I asked her to sit for a while and she did. She was always the mother and friend.
>
> The second image is of her quietness. I am a kindred spirit here as I am also referred to as being quiet. In a house full of seven children, six vociferous girls, eight grandchildren she was there listening and absorbing and knowing. She did not need to speak all the time. She loved what she did had a passion for doing anything to make family and friends at ease and at home. Her home. She was always the mother and friend.

After the birth of our first child, our son Viruben, I opted to leave the field job and get a job at the GEC offices in Coventry. I commuted daily from Northampton to Coventry, about an hour's drive on the motorway. After a few years of the long commute from Northampton to Coventry, I applied for a job in a consulting firm called Ewbank Preece in Brighton and was offered the job. We decided to sell up in Northampton and move south.

At Ewbank Preece, I got involved in a new area of telecommunications.

In 1962, the world's first active-communications satellite, Telstar 1, was launched. This satellite was built by AT&T and Bell Laboratories as a collaboration with the British post office and French post office. During its short lifespan of seven months in operation, Telstar 1 dazzled the world with live images of sports, entertainment, and news. It was a simple, single-transponder, low-earth-orbit (LEO) satellite, but its technology of receiving radio signals from the ground and then amplifying and retransmitting them over a large portion of the earth's surface set the standard for all communications satellites that followed.

The technology continued to develop during the '70s, and satellites were put into a geostationary orbit. This was an orbit that made the satellite look stationary to the ground station on earth, a concept first put forward by Arthur Clarke. In 1975, HBO began distributing its video programs via satellite to its customers.

In the 1980s, the Arab League of Nations resolved to have a regional satellite that they would launch and operate to facilitate communication between their members. Ewbank Preece was appointed as consultants to implement ground stations in three of the poorer countries of the league, Mauritania, Djibouti, and South Yemen.

I was new to this field and had to learn fast.

I was working under Dr. Khider Buni an Iraqi who had settled in England. He was extremely knowledgeable in the subject and was prepared to share his knowledge. I learnt fast and had to visit France and Japan for doing the acceptance testing of the all the equipment before it was shipped. The main contractors were NEC of Japan and Thompson from France.

I successfully completed the commissioning of the earth stations at Djibouti and Mauritania and had returned back to UK. The earth station in Aden, South Yemen, was being installed and getting ready for the final testing and commissioning.

In 1980, the People's Democratic Republic of Yemen's President Abdul Ismail resigned and went into exile in Moscow. He had lost the support and confidence of his sponsors in the Soviet Union.

The year was 1986. The Berlin Wall was still standing. Gorbachev was the leader of the USSR.

Margret Thatcher was into her second term as prime minister. That year the French and British governments announced that they would construct a channel tunnel connecting the two countries. It was to be opened in the early '90s.

In January 1986, a few months before I had to go to South Yemen, a violent struggle began in Aden between the supporters of the successor to Abdul Ismail, President Ali Nasir, and supporters of the returned Ismail, who wanted power back. The Yemen civil war started and lasted more than a month. There were thousands of casualties, and Ali Nasir was ousted and Ismail was killed.

Although this was a civil war, it was news in Britain. The war was in the news as the queen's yacht, the Royal Yacht *Britannia*, was in Aden. As it was leaving Aden, it was redirected and used for the evacuation of the British expatriates and families living there. They were evacuated from the beach, quite close to the place where the earth station was being built.

In February that year, we were living in Peacehaven, a small village on the southern coast of England close to Brighton. There is rarely snow in Brighton most years. That particular year was really cold in February, with heavy snow and subzero temperatures.

Viruben, our son, was two years and eight months. Sharadha, my wife, was heavily pregnant with our second child. I had planned to drive her to the hospital, as I had done for the birth of our son, when she went into labour. With the heavy storm, snow had covered the coastal road, and it was strongly advised that everyone stay indoors. My daughter thought otherwise. Quite in keeping with her character, she decided she wanted to start her life outside the womb, right then, during this freak storm in Brighton.

We had to call for an ambulance and have a neighbour take care of our son. Naomi was born on a cold, snowy day in February that year.

The news from South Yemen was not good, but things had settled a bit. We were committed to the project, and the Japanese contractors were ready for the testing. We had this newborn baby and young son. I was concerned leaving the family. We requested some help from the extended family in Colombo, and Tushara, my wife's sister, came over to Peacehaven to spend some time and help out with the two young children.

I left shortly after that for Aden in South Yemen to commission the earth station to the ARABSAT satellite. The evidence of the civil war was everywhere. The country was still tense. We had to repair several bullet holes in the large satellite-receiving dish. The job took several months, and I remained there, living in a very basic hotel, with very limited meal options.

Ewbank Preece was tasked by the Australian government to do a study on the use of their radio frequency spectrum. The company had just completed a similar study in the UK. I was asked to join the team as the technical expert. This was my first trip to Australia.

Our assignment took us to Melbourne, Brisbane, Sydney, and Canberra. I fell in love with the open spaces, the weather, and the lesser formality of the people. In particular I liked the harbour city of Sydney. The seed was sowed on that trip. If there was any opportunity, I wanted to move my family and live here.

On my return from that trip, I applied for immigration to Australia. The process took a long time, and I gradually lost hope that the application would progress and conclude. The move to Sydney seemed more and more a distant dream. We got on with our life.

The dawn of competition was just about to begin in telecommunications.

It was an exciting time for our industry that had been so closed and always a government monopoly. The wave of deregulation had begun in the USA. AT&T was broken up, and new companies Sprint and MCI were showing the way on how prices could be reduced for the consumer.

In Britain, the consortium called Mercury Communications won the license to set up and operate an alternate service to British Telecom. I applied for a job as a senior project manager with this new company and was given a role in London. Just as I received the letter of offer from Mercury, I also received word from the Australian High Commission in London suggesting that I had made the cut, and they wanted to know if I wanted to take the migration process to the next level and complete the formalities. It was an agonising decision.

We were comfortable in our home in Peacehaven. The children were young, Naomi still a baby. They were both healthy kids who were enjoying their surroundings. We had plenty of friends, and family to visit at weekends in London. Most of London was an hour-and-a-half drive away. We had a comfortable detached house in Peacehaven. We were happy with the schools around Peacehaven. It was close to the sea, a short drive to Brighton, a short drive to Eastbourne.

I was excited about my new job. I was given a large and complex project to do. Mercury had to build their whole network from scratch. British Telecom was not going to give any help. New international gateways had to be built to handle overseas telephone calls. I was tasked with project managing the building of the International Earth Station for Mercury at Whitehill in Oxfordshire.

I decided to decline taking the next steps for the migration to Australia.

The company, Mercury, were doing well. A new operations HQ was to be built to bring all the different divisions into one purpose made building. They chose to make this HQ in Bracknell in Berkshire. We were all given attractive packages to move closer to the new HQ. Travelling to London had been easy from Peacehaven, I used to drive to the station and take the fast train into London every day. It would not be possible to commute from Peacehaven to Bracknell.

We sold up in Peacehaven and moved to Wokingham.

The company was expanding rapidly. I was comfortable and settled. At about that time, reading the Sunday papers, I came across a job advertisement for project managers in Sydney, Australia. Reading the advertisement rekindled the desire for the life I had seen possible in Sydney. I applied.

My experience with Mercury had added something more to my CV. This made it immensely attractive to OTC, the Overseas Telecommunication Commission of Australia, the government-owned, monopoly operator of all international phone calls in and out of Australia, who were recruiting in the UK.

The agent interviewed me on the M4 motorway service station at Heston; we had a coffee and a long chat. He was convinced enough to put forward my name for an interview with the panel who were coming down from Australia to make the selections. I attended the interview with the panel and was selected.

Again, I was confronted with this choice. I had applied for the job, not knowing what to expect and certainly would not have been too disappointed had I not got the job.

What do I do?

I had already decided that if I ever get to Australia, I would prefer the harbour city of Sydney. Here was a job offered in Sydney. It was a job with an Australian government-owned entity. No risk there. It was fully assisted; my passage and that of the family was paid. We were given accommodation for a few weeks till we sorted ourselves out, and all the assistance we needed to settle in this new world. Yet I recall it was a tough choice.

The job being offered was two levels below my job level in Mercury Communications.

The generation before me, my parents' generation, were comfortable with the notion of joining a company or the government service and staying there for the duration of their working life. They worked themselves up the ladder in the same industry or profession until they reached their peak. When they started their decline—either because the world had changed; technology had come in; younger, more alert people were knocking on their door—it was time to retire anyway.

However, today, the pace of life is getting faster, and we are moving along the career path at a much faster speed. This means that in my generation and generations after me, we cannot expect to be in one organisation for all our working life. We would have reached our peak much faster. The world and circumstances would have changed quickly to make all the experience we had gained irrelevant, and we would be quickly in decline. The accelerating pace of change shrinks our careers in a particular organisation. The organisation would, in fact, boot us out if we arrogantly stayed, thinking we were indispensable.

As Charles Handy explains in his book *The Empty Raincoat*, the secret of constant growth is to start a new career before the first one reaches its peak. The secret is to recognise where you are on the career curve, to be aware of the world and the changing circumstances around you, and to make the change early enough so there is time as well as resources and energy to get the new curve through its initial fumbling and learning.

However, this is easier said than done. It is at this very precise time when you are reaching your peak that everything and all messages come through that you or the organisation is doing really well. The last thing on your mind at this time is to make a change. The advice is, "if it's working, don't change it."

Sometimes when we change jobs, we need to take drop in our grade, to learn a new skill, to prove ourselves yet again in a new organisation. This is the time we may be at a lower point from where we were had we continued in our older job or role. The upside will come, as we learn the new skills and we start the new curve taking us to even greater heights.

I had fought hard to get to this senior manager position in UK. There was the racial bias I had to overcome, the glass ceiling. I had fought to get to that place. In the '80s, at the age of thirty-four, this was good. People knew me in the company; I had established my credentials.

Having completed the two earth stations on time and budget, I was given the task of connecting the submarine cable link that landed in Cornwall from the USA to the international exchange.

This was an optical fibre link, a brand-new technology. This was a time when optical fibre was only just being deployed in Europe. I was entrusted with this major project in this young and vibrant company. The family was settled and happy; the children spoke with strong English accents.

Our house in Barkham was a detached, four-bedroom house on the corner of a cul-de-sac in a new and secure, gated community. We were hardly an hour away from London on the M4, and our very good friends whom I had known since childhood, with three children of their own, were living a few minutes away.

The housing market was down in the dumps in UK, and I could not sell my house. I certainly would get less than what I paid for the house if I could sell it, but there were no buyers. The interest rates in Australia were an astronomical 17 percent, and yet the housing market in Sydney was strong. Sydney real estate prices were high. It was the wrong time to move, if one were moving assets from the UK to Australia.

If the decision was hard for me, it was harder for Sharadha, my wife. She had close family, a sister Keshini, who was just starting her family, uncles and aunts and cousins, all within one- to two-hour drive from our home. She was concerned. She had not seen Australia. I had to show confidence to her that this was the right move for all of us.

The tough choice was eventually made; we decided to take the risk, open this door. I decided to start a new curve, dropping a few levels down, in the hope that this new curve would propel me to a higher orbit.

Once we made our minds, we did not look back. We made arrangements to move and bid our farewells.

We left England, that warm and bright day in early June 1989. It was a hot summer that year; England was glorious in the heat. This added to the agony of leaving our abode for the past fifteen years. We decided to travel to Australia via the USA, spend a few days with my sister Shalini and her family, and spend a few days in LA and Hawaii before heading to Sydney.

I arrived in Sydney in that June of 1989 and started work as a project manager in OTC Australia.

In November that year, the Berlin Wall was broken down.

OTC was a monopoly company, owned by the government of Australia. I was assigned to the engineering group and within that to a projects division in the company.

I had handled much larger projects in England, but this was Australia, and one had to start at a lower level and had to prove oneself in this new environment before one could aspire to bigger things. Around the same time I joined OTC, a new business division was created to explore opportunities overseas. The telecommunications industry was deregulating slowly, and some licences were being offered in different countries for partners such as OTC to be involved and to invest. OTC International was created to explore these opportunities.

The head of OTCI was Peter Shore. Peter was a bit like one of my favourite bosses in England, John Mittens. Peter had charisma, was intelligent and incisive, and was approachable. He was generous with his time, always available despite his position in the organisation, and he was fun. You instinctively knew he was a leader you wanted to follow.

OTC was a typical engineering company with the cardigan-wearing, gentle but conservative management team in all the leadership positions. You moved up the rank in this organisation based on mileage in the company, loyalty, age, and being favoured by your boss.

Peter was not an engineer; he was a journalist, a teacher in his past career before getting into management. He believed in people.

OTCI was staffed by ex-diplomats and others from outside the telecom industry. For me, this was a breath of fresh air. I closely tracked the progress of OTCI projects, and by lobbying at the right time, I made sure I was assigned as a project manager to OTCI projects.

I decided that I needed to study marketing to expand my horizon beyond this engineering focus. I enrolled in night classes and got my qualification. My love of travel led me to posture and lobby heavily to be the "technical person" of choice when accompanying the business development team on their overseas visits to drum up business. This relationship with the business heads made me get even closer to some of the key decision-makers in OTCI. I travelled extensively during this period to the Pacific islands, Croatia, Azerbaijan, Kazakhstan, and many other places.

The year was 1992. The Berlin Wall had fallen in 1989. President Tito of Yugoslavia had passed away, and the independence wars of the various ethnic groups that made up that country had commenced.

OTC International was looking at opportunities in the newly emerging countries. There were many migrants from the Balkans in Australia, and the international telephone traffic to these countries was high. The war was still raging on.

We had a particularly strong lead in Croatia, and I was asked to travel there. Croatia needed to have independent international communications with the outside world; they were in need of investment and help.

Croatia wished to leave Yugoslavia and become a sovereign country, while many ethnic Serbs living in Croatia, supported by Serbia, opposed the secession and wanted Croatia to remain a part of Yugoslavia. I was to fly into Zagreb, but the fighting meant the flight could not land there, and the plane was diverted to Ljubljana (pronounced *Loo-blyah-na*), the capital of Slovenia.

Slovenia had recently been declared independent. The only way to get from the airport at Ljubljana to Zagreb was by bus. The distance was about 150 Km. The bus was very basic and not comfortable. As we drove along the mountainous, narrow roads, we could see the devastation of the war; there was still fighting going on. It was a tense ride to Zagreb. In Zagreb, I was treated well. I was invited to the president's palace for meetings. The mood and the atmosphere were tense. You could feel that after many years of communist rule, the people were wanting change, wanting their independence, but were fearful of authority. The Croatian war of independence that had started in 1991 lasted for four years and ended in 1995.

In the early '90s, deregulation of the telecommunications fixed-line telephone service was gathering steam. One of the big issues facing the new entrants was how to provide the last mile connection to the home. This was the big advantage of the incumbent government-owned telephone operators. They would not share this key competitive edge they had. Mobile phones were still in the research-and-development phase. Wireless was clearly the answer. A new digital technology called CT2 was invented and starting to be deployed. CT2 is a cordless telephony standard that was used to provide short-range pseudo-mobile phone service in some countries in Europe. A service called Rabbit was launched in UK.

Hong Kong decided to issue three licenses for this new service. OTC International decided to join a local company, the Chevalier Group, and make a bid. When the opportunity for a manager to go to Hong Kong to evaluate this new business opportunity came up, I was asked to go. It meant leaving the family. I agreed on the basis that I could come back every two weeks. We won the bid, and I was asked to project manage the setting up of the new venture. The company was formed, and I was appointed as managing director of the company. At the age of thirty-seven, I had broken through the glass ceiling.

The task was my first start-up, setting up the company from scratch. We had a target launch date for the service and frantically worked to get the brand, distribution channels, and pricing all fixed. We had to negotiate with shop owners and street corners for access to attach a small base station on the external wall. The base station had a very small range, and you could only make calls standing close to the base station. It was basically a cordless base station that could support many handsets.

After six months, OTC International had appointed Neil Montefiore as the new MD of this venture, and I returned to Sydney. Neil went on to be CEO of M1 and then Star Hub in Singapore.

It was 1992. I had returned to my role in OTC International in Sydney. OTC was a great place to work. It had a real family feel to the company. George Maltby had set the standards, the values, and the culture. He had risen from being a post boy, taking mail from the post room to people's desks, to be the CEO of the company. Steve Burdon replaced George when he retired. I had hosted Steve in Hong Kong when he came to visit and had got to know him. It was very open style of management. Everyone was in the same building, and we had a great canteen where we could all meet and mingle during lunch. It was the best place I had worked in, and the culture was one I tried to replicate in my subsequent roles as leader.

The queen visited Australia that year, and Paul Keating, the prime minister, broke protocol by placing his hand gently on the queen's back. This caused an outraged British tabloids to name him the "Lizard of Oz." The Cricket World Cup was hosted by Australia and New Zealand that year. Imran Khan's Pakistan team beat England in the finals. It was the first World Cup to be played under lights and with coloured clothing.

We had settled well in the new country, and I had concluded that this was the best decision I had made. The risk had paid off. I now called Australia home. We applied and got our citizenship.

Things were changing at OTC. Two years earlier, in a cabinet decision, the Hawke government decided to merge Telecom Australia and OTC to form one large company and then to sell off Aussat, which was debt laden, to a new player. This was to be a duopoly market.

The changes had begun, and Telecom Australia also had an international division looking for opportunities overseas. This was merged with OTC International where I worked. I had some new bosses and new colleagues.

This was a merger between a giant Telecom Australia that had around 90,000 employees and a minnow OTC that had 2,000 employees. There was a lot of jostling for key positions, people taking early retirement, a lot of people joining the new Aussat organisation, later to become Optus.

A new toll road to be called the M2 had been planned to be built from Lane Cove to the western suburbs of Sydney. The land required for building the road included part of our front garden. We received a letter that our home was to be acquired.

In a way, this was good news. The road had been planned for thirty years, and it was on all maps, marked as a dotted line. A wide corridor of land had been left, and this was full of large gum trees. We had enjoyed the privacy and the greenery this forest had provided in front of our house. The consensus was that since for thirty years no government had the money or inclination to build this road, it would never be built. We certainly bought the property on that assumption. We were aware that the value of the property had taken this factor that a road may be built into account. If the road were built as planned on the map, we would not have had been offered any compensation. Instead of a quiet cul-de-sac, we would be living in front of a major highway.

However, for our luck, the new plan of the road included a toll gate, entrance, and exit, which meant more land was needed, and this land required included part of our home. Since this was a change to the original planned land corridor, they were compelled to acquire us.

That year, OTC International were invited to bid for a license to operate a mobile communications network in Sri Lanka. One must appreciate that this did not generate a lot of excitement or enthusiasm in the office. Mobile communications was in its infancy. No one imagined the impact and the size the industry would grow to at that time. No one imagined it would surpass the fixed-line numbers in all countries. Telecom Australia had a small mobile network working on the analogue US standard called AMPS. There were two competing standards at the time globally—the US standard and the European standard called ETACS. The service in Australia was restricted to the major cities.

Everyone was expecting this to be another paging-type business, never to be a challenger to the fixed phones.

Those who could afford it would carry the large brick phone; some had car phones. Some car phones were fixed. Others were able to be removed from the car, and you could walk around with it. It was the size of a briefcase. The battery was large and heavy. It was easy to see how this was not going to be a consumer product. It was a product for a limited few. The call charges and other fees made it a luxury product.

Sri Lanka too was not a desired destination. Ranasinghe Premadasa was the president of Sri Lanka. He had attempted peace negotiations with the Liberation Tigers of Tamil Eelam (LTTE), popularly known as the Tigers, and this had failed. What was known as Eelam War II had commenced. With the war on in the country, no one was keen to go there.

It was just as we were digesting the news of the new road and coming to terms that we would have to move from our existing residence in Sydney and search for a new home that the opportunity in Colombo was being discussed in the office, and my possibility of being posted to Colombo came up.

There were no guarantees we would be successful in our bid. The approvals were not all done, but the merged company, now called Telstra, needed someone on the ground to keep things moving, to attend to all the start-up activities, such as setting up the company and developing a business plan.

I volunteered.

It was not an easy decision. We had only arrived in Australia three years before. Our home was under the threat of acquisition for the new M2 motorway and what compensation we would get for the home was not clear. We sought and appointed a firm of solicitors to represent us during our absence.

The weekend before we left for Sri Lanka on our new assignment, we saw this newspaper advertisement advertising that some plots of land were available in our suburb of Beecroft. Beecroft is a well-established, mature suburb, and the availability of new land is rare. We had many things to do before we left for Colombo, and in spite of the rush, we drove down this steep lane called Timbertop Way that Saturday afternoon just before the closing time advertised. Everything else seemed great about this spot. It was off Malton Road, a wide, tree-lined boulevard with large, established houses. It was walking distance to the Beecroft station and the village shops, once you had climbed this steep hill. We knew the price would be very high; we just thought we would drop by, out of curiosity.

The salesperson was about to close up. This was a fire sale; the developer had gone bust, and the bank was now selling the plots to recover some money. There were eleven plots for sale. Some had already been sold. We had a quick look at the plots available and picked the plot on which our home now stands. The salesman said the plot was taken. A young couple who were interested had just gone to consult their architect; because of the slope of the land they needed some assurances about the cost of building before placing a deposit.

I had a choice—walk away or make the deposit and think on how to solve the funding and building later. I had this letter from the state wanting to acquire my property for the toll road, but I had no idea when that would conclude. We had no idea of the compensation they would offer. There was a risk that it might not conclude and the project would fail. The government had a habit of promising these large infrastructure projects and cancelling them due to lack of funds. They may not succeed in acquiring all the land needed for the new road.

The price of the land was high in Beecroft compared to the newer, neighbouring suburbs; it was a large commitment that I would have to make. I already had a mortgage and would have to increase that. But the price of the land in this particular site was being offered lower than the market rate, because it was a fire sale. Land in Beecroft was expensive. The deposit required to make him put a sold sign was around $500.

I had no time to go home and get my cheque book. I had a $50 note in my purse. I gave it to him and persuaded the salesperson to put the sold sign up, that I would settle him the balance on Monday. He did.

We were in a state of shock when we got home that evening. It had been a choice made in haste, but we had a very narrow window of opportunity.

I held the land for three years, during which time our existing property eventually got acquired by the government.

We built our current home on this plot of land. We completed the construction just after we returned from my assignment as managing director of Mobitel in Sri Lanka.

We still call this place home. It was the only home we had kept and lived in for so long. It is the place where the children grew up, the place where my daughter Naomi left as a bride, where my son Viruben left as a bridegroom.

The deck and the view, the quiet, the birds that frequent the reserve at the back, I love everything about this home.

Chapter 7

Mobitel. Now You're Talking ...

I was standing by the window of my suite at the Colombo Ramada Hotel, staring at the Beira Lake. The hotel is now known as the Cinnamon Lakeside. The children and Sharadha were down by the pool. I was tense and disappointed.

I had just heard that the final approval for the licence needed to operate a mobile network in Sri Lanka had not been considered at the cabinet meeting of the Sri Lankan government. It was on the agenda but had been missed. I had a strong suspicion there were persons working against us getting the approval. I had moved over from Sydney with the whole family. I wondered if I had I taken too much of a risk, uprooting my family from the comfort of Sydney to come here to Colombo, Sri Lanka.

The OTC International team had made many visits to Colombo; they had been successful in winning the tender initiated by Sri Lanka Telecom to provide a nationwide mobile-telephone service in the country. They had most of the approvals done, and one remained. What remained was a mere formality, the final cabinet approval from the government. I was asked to head the initial project team in setting up the mobile network. At that time, there was no commitment given or assumed that I would be the managing director of the company.

There was a ship on the high seas, making its way from Australia to Colombo with the mobile-switching exchange. We informed Ericsson, the supplier, that the license was a formality; we had asked them to ship the equipment so we didn't waste time. I had made promises and assurances to my bosses in Australia that all was well. The approval was listed on the agenda for the cabinet meeting. Officials at the Ministry of Post and Communications had assured me it would be taken up and approved.

Unbeknown to me, other forces were at work.

Singapore Telecom had recently been awarded a license, and they had commenced the building of their network infrastructure, the service to be called Call Link. The technology was based on the European mobile standard ETACS. They had yet to launch their service.

We intended to adopt a different technology, our network based on the US standard AMPS. The incumbent Celltel, owned by Millicom International, were also on the European ETACS standard.

We were at the infancy of mobile communication globally. Sri Lanka was the first South Asian country with mobile phones. The AMPS and ETACS were analogue standards that preceded the digital GSM standard. The difference to the users was in the phones. The AMPS phone would not work on the ETACS network and vice versa.

The sec to the ministry of finance, Paskaralingam, was extremely powerful in the Premadasa government, and the competition used their influence to lobby their position that two operators, Celltel and Call Link, were more than sufficient for the market. Everyone was opposed to Sri Lanka Telecom having its own mobile network.

There was a view that SLT should stick to the fixed-line telephone business and not venture into this new technology of mobile phones.

During the bidding, the OTC International team led by John Lilywhite had made many visits and had made presentations to Sri Lanka Telecom and many of the other ministries. We were assisted by Austrade and the Australian high commission in arranging meetings with the government officials. It made sense to use Austrade, as we were an Australian government-owned organisation. John and I had got to know Howard Debenham, the high commissioner, very well.

When this block happened, I had to mobilise and do my own lobbying.

The next day, I contacted senior officials at Austrade and the Ministry of Post and Communications. I had been regularly keeping the high commission informed on the progress of Telstra's venture to operate a mobile Network on behalf of Sri Lanka Telecom.

This was a very large investment by an Australian government-owned entity into Sri Lanka. Sri Lanka ravaged by the war in the north desperately wanted to attract investment into the country. The board of Telstra were concerned about the risk of investing in Sri Lanka and could pull the plug anytime.

I had to get this resolved. After a few meetings with the Ministry of Finance to resolve certain misunderstandings, we had everyone satisfied. A few weeks later, we received the cabinet approval required to proceed.

The high commissioner later wrote to Peter Shore, the managing director of Telstra International in Australia, commending me and my colleague, John Lillywhite, on the professional and diligent way we handled the whole approval process.

One has to imagine that in 1992 mobiles were not as prevalent as they are today. The phones were the size of a brick; they cost the equivalent of a gold coin and were the purview of a privileged few.

The company, Celltel, had been operating in Sri Lanka for four years and had coverage of only greater Colombo. They were running a monopoly service. It was a service for the privileged few. There was not a single mobile phone in India, Pakistan, or Bangladesh. Australia had its own mobile service but was also limited in coverage and the cost of calls prohibitive. It was universally accepted at that time that mobiles would remain a tool for the rich. The market projections for a developing country like Sri Lanka were small. In the scheme of things within Telstra, this was a very small project.

I had left Sri Lanka eighteen years before to pursue my higher education in England. I had visited the country a few times for holidays. I had got married in Colombo. Except for the first job I held, I had no experience of working there. I certainly did not have the relationships and contacts in the business and corporate community. Accepting the assignment was a choice with many risks. Failure would mean more humiliation than failing in Australia, for example, as it was in front of the family and the small, tight community.

I had no experience in this new mobile phone technology; very few did at that time. I had to learn and adapt as I went along. I was an expat in the country of my parents, but as far as setting up a business goes, I was as familiar to the process and had very few contacts in the business world, as would any other Aussie expat sent to Colombo. The financial compensation was no real incentive; government-owned organisations made very little changes to your Australian pay when they sent you overseas.

There were many candidates aspiring to be managing director of Mobitel in Sri Lanka, many who were more qualified than me within Telstra. There was no guarantee given to me that I would be the managing director of this new company. My role was to set up the company and build the network as a project. I was determined though to make the MD role mine. My tenacity and my initial work in getting approvals in the country helped; having just done a stint in Hong Kong as managing director also helped.

The choice of who would be MD, though, ultimately would be made by those in Sydney. None of these factors would really have mattered. There was pressure from the mobile division within Telstra that they had the right to appoint the managing director. They wanted someone who was familiar with this new mobile technology. They wanted one of their own to be in charge.

The internal battles and politics were intense. The recent merger between the larger Telecom Australia and the smaller OTC caused many territorial battles, and these were still being played out. The mobile division was from Telecom Australia. OTC had won the license in Sri Lanka. I was on the ground, getting things done, oblivious to the politics back in Australia.

I focussed on getting things done. I did not pay attention to the politics. I knew that results mattered. I also realized that it is about who you know, the relationships and trust you develop with people who matter. I had developed and cultivated good relations with the people who I reported to and who mattered. I kept them informed and made them aware of the progress I was making. My belief is that it was the combination of my focus, my taking responsibility, and getting on with the job that eventually made it happen.

The appointment came. I was the CEO and managing director of Telstra's first mobile service outside of Australia, the founding managing director of Mobitel. At thirty-seven, I had reached the "C" floor. All the choices and risks had paid off.

A small team joined me from Australia to help with the set up. Ed Koh was the financial expert, Peter Zerna, the technical expert, and Ray was to help me with the sales and marketing. We initially set up an office in two of the rooms at the Ramada Hotel. We had numerous others from the Telstra team in Australia who would visit and help out as we set up the company. Among them, visiting frequently, were Kalinga Wijewardene, who was the legal expert; Karl Matacz and Cathy Aston from finance; and John Lilywhite, who I reported to. Everyone contributed to ensuring the company was set up and we had funding in place. Cathy later became CEO of Mobitel in 1998.

We got on with setting up the chart of accounts, building the network, and evaluating sales and distribution partners. As the American AMPS standard was being used, we had to bring in new hand phones. The existing phones in the country working on the Celltel network could not work on our network. Our strategy had to appeal to a new segment of the market; the phones had to be cheaper to own, and the call charges had to be lower.

We encouraged the representatives of Motorola and Nokia to talk to local companies. We made the introductions to Tito Pestonjee and Dinesh Ambani of the Abans Group and the Metropolitan Group. We set up a scheme of subsidising the handset price to make it more affordable for the market.

I had located a new building close to the Beira Lake in Colombo that would be suitable for our offices. I set up a few boxes on the empty concrete floor as we got contractors to quote on the fitting out for the furniture, ceilings, and floor covers. I conducted interviews for the new team in this dusty, cavernous environment. There was no mistaking to anyone attending an interview that this was a start-up. We had run full-page advertisements in the newspapers for all of the top positions. I had spent my whole day sifting through the CVs. I was looking for people who would embrace the pioneering spirit. Yes, they would be joining an Australian company, but that was all I was promising. The rest was a gamble; this could work out or not.

We worked with Zenith Advertising and Kenneth Honter. I had already decided the name Mobitel. We developed the logo, in the colours of OTC, blue and grey. Guy Halpe came up with the tag line: "Now you're talking." This was brilliant. We were entering a monopoly market, the second player. The emphasis was on the *now*. Now things were going to change.

Gradually we built the senior team that was to take the country by storm. Most of them not from the telecoms industry. I was urged by my Australian colleagues to take those from the industry.

My instincts were telling me otherwise. I looked into the consumer-marketing industry for my sales and marketing head. Sunil joined me and learnt fast. The engineering head, Wijeya, was working at Celltel and was frustrated that he could not progress in that company. He approached me to explore the possibilities of heading the engineering team, and I grabbed him. This was a real coup. There were very few engineers who had experience in building this new technology called *mobiles* globally. I wanted to build a local team. Others joined to make up the senior team. Ranadev as CFO and Peter as human resources head, Lalith as head of IT. Jean joined to lead the customer service team.

I recruited Natali as my PA from the hospitality industry.

With all my direct reports, I wanted a team that had no preconceptions about the roles they were about to take. I did not want anyone to come with a blinkered view about how things would be done.

I wanted all of them to have a hunger for learning the new role and responsibilities. They all had their special skills, but the culture and values, the soul of the team, I would coach and inculcate.

Some mistakes were also made. It was inevitable that in the rush we would make mistakes, but the essential lesson was that we learnt, and we moved on. Speed was key. Wallowing and analysing mistakes would waste time.

To help me with this book and to give a different perspective, I recently asked Natali to pen a few words of the time she was at Mobitel.

> I presume Vijay believed that I could assist him as his PA when I walked through the MD's office door of Mobitel in 1994 to face the preliminary interview. The interview was very professional and to the point. I was selected, and it was great to work for the MD of Mobitel owned by OTC Australia.
>
> The entire Mobitel pioneering team was handpicked by Vijay. He made time available to interview each candidate and also made sure that all references were checked before hiring. He did not make any mistakes on the persons who came on board. The staff morale was at its peak.
>
> The procedure followed for board meetings was absolutely professional. The agenda was prepared and sent out to the board of directors along with the board papers, which were well documented. The MD's report was the highlight of many meetings. The board of directors of OTC Australia and Sri Lanka Telecom had a very high regard for Vijay. They knew that the company was in good hands.

I was supposed to keep an up-to-date diary when we did not have the privilege of online diaries in the bygone era. I also recall how annoyed Vijay got when a travel arrangement in the USA had not been followed-up by me with the travel agent properly and he had to face issues once he landed in the USA. It made me realize that any work which had to be coordinated through a third party had to be followed-up and not to take things for granted. I also will not forget the travel file he used to carry with him on many overseas trips on business. The file had to be up-to-date with the itinerary/details of the hotel/any other important documents, etc.

We caught everyone by surprise when we launched the Mobitel service in April 1993.

We had built up expectations before the launch, and there was a pent up demand. Within a month, we had 500 connections. This number might seem very small now, but back then it was a huge number. Very few people could afford a mobile phone.

I was surprised. My colleagues in Australia were surprised.

In less than six months, we had built the network with sufficient coverage in Colombo to match Celltel, the competitor, and decided to surprise the market. No one expected that we could roll out the network in such a short time. Call Link, owned by Singapore Telecom, had started over a year earlier with big plans and were still building their network. They had not counted on us launching so soon. They were caught completely by surprise, as was the incumbent Celltel.

I learnt then the value of speed. This became our DNA.

We were using some of Sri Lanka Telecom's existing infrastructure as part of the project, and that helped us to a great extent. However, Sri Lanka Telecom was still a government-owned corporation and getting things done, even though they were partners, was slow and painful. A great team from Australia and locally recruited engineers, some who took early retirement from SLT and joined us, all just came together and worked day and night, building towers, testing, and retesting to get a basic network up and running that we could launch with.

The time of our launch, April 1993, was not a good time in Sri Lanka.

A former minister in the government, Lalith Athulathmudali, was assassinated at a political rally in Colombo. There was tension in the air as the president of the country at that time, Premadasa, was suspected of being involved. The two of them, Lalith and Premedasa, had been ministerial colleagues in the previous government, and both were contenders for the nomination to contest the presidency. Premadasa was chosen and subsequently won the election. After his victory as president, he ostracised his two rivals, Lalith and Gamini Dissanayake in the ruling party. They both eventually left the ruling party to form their own party in opposition. The war with the LTTE from the north of the country was still raging on. The body of a Tamil youth was found the next day, and the blame was placed on this youth for the assassination of Lalith.

The president vehemently denied his involvement, saying, "Assassinate me if you wish, but don't assassinate my character."

On May 1, a few weeks later, during the May Day rally, a suicide bomber got close to President Premadasa, despite his high security, and blew himself up. President Premadasa and many of his security personnel and close associates were killed.

The situation in the country was dire. Telstra in Australia was concerned for their investment. The team from Australia who was helping me wanted to get out. I was left on my own, with the local team.

We created a lot of buzz in the market with our launch, and within a few days, we had a response from Celltel none of us imagined was possible.

Full-page advertisements in all the newspapers screamed *free* phones from Celltel. There were queues forming outside their office, people eager to get these free phones. The technology we used for Mobitel was different from that of both Celltel and Call Link, and so our mobile phones were unique. We could not offer the service to the Celltel customer who would come in and want to use the same handset with a new number. We had offered very reasonably priced handsets in the market and were getting new users to our service.

The cream of high-end customers was still with Celltel. They wanted to keep it that way. By offering a free handset to existing customers, they were ensuring the loyalty to continue. Anyone bringing a Mobitel handset was being offered two free handsets. They were trying to kill us at birth.

This was a baptism of fire for me, introduction to intense competition and also to consumer marketing.

We had a choice to ignore the campaign or to fight back and take it to another level, stare each other down so to speak, destroying value in the market as a result. It was a tough call.

Ultimately we decided to take up the fight. We wanted to project an image as an aggressive competitor that just awoke the monopoly provider who had been fleecing the customer with high call charges.

We wanted to take the moral high ground as the champion of the consumer. We wanted to live the tag line, "Now you're talking…"

We immediately took full-page advertisements with the campaign, "More than just a *free* phone." We packaged a number of other goodies with it and virtually killed their campaign.

The phone wars continued, daily full-page advertisements in the newspapers. No one imagined that this mundane, ordinary communications industry could get so consumer-driven and so competitive. It was exciting times. I was thoroughly engaged and took a keen interest in building a close and motivated team. I was up at 4:00 a.m. each morning, preparing for the day ahead. At 6:30 a.m. I would head from our apartment to the Colombo Cricket Club (CCC) grounds a short walk away and jog for an hour. This was my daily routine.

I enjoyed these morning walks at the CCC. It was the only exercise I got. I enjoyed it more, though, for the friends I made and the conversations we had during that time. We were a mixed bunch, some eminent national sports persons and successful businessmen and me. Michael S. was a partner in the law firm we had engaged to set up Mobitel, and so I knew him; he was always first there. Vijaya M. was a director at Ceylon Tobacco, was always last. Both had played cricket for their respective schools and Ceylon. Jayantha J. was a rugby legend and Trinity Lion. A global expert on the conservation of wild elephants, JJA was an owner-director of the Metropolitan Group, a large conglomerate, and Sanka W. was a director at the Ceylinco Group. He was always travelling and had tales to relate of his exploits abroad.

The conversations were lively and full of wit. We were occasionally joined by PSK, a former national tennis champion and one who had a host of new stories to relate.

The team's hard work at Mobitel was paying off. We were a strong contender to Celltell. We had left Call Link in third place. The business was so successful that we met the targets in customer numbers of the seven-year business plan in two years.

One of Mobitel's unique propositions and the reason it was so successful was the pioneering of mobile communications to towns outside of Colombo. We were the first to provide mobile communications to Matara, Anuradhapura, Chilaw and many other towns in the country.

The launch in Chilaw has special memories for me. It was the town where my father-in-law was a prominent doctor, lion, and personality. Albert had served the town and its people for 40 years as a doctor and leader. I sensed his pride in front of the other doctors and guests on that day of the launch. Albert passed away in 2010.

We had become the second-largest mobile operator in two years and were very close to Celltel that had been operating for six years. The original deal between SLT and Telstra was a seven-year build-operate-and-transfer (BOT). The investment was fixed, and it was hoped the business would make a certain return for Telstra so that it recovered its initial investment plus return and handover to SLT an operation they could takeover in 2000.

The success meant the company needed new investment. It needed investment to expand the network and expand capacity as the customer numbers were growing faster than planned. To the credit of both SLT and Telstra, they reacted quickly. The network was overloaded, and calls were dropping while customers were talking. Customers could not get on the network to make a call, as it was busy. We had built a reputation of good service and that reputation was being eroded. The tag line "Now you're talking" seemed a bit lame.

The billing system we had from Australia was very basic and could not cope with the volume of customers we were having. Lalith, the IT head, and Saman from our IT team said they could build a new billing system from scratch. The quotes from reputable companies was prohibitive. I took a gamble and asked them to proceed. It paid off. Saman built a great and flexible billing system that gave us a competitive edge.

The teams from Telstra and SLT negotiated a better deal. It resulted in changing Mobitel from a BOT to a joint venture, where Telstra owned 60 percent of the company and SLT owned 40 percent of the company. The new injection of capital allowed us to invest and grow nationwide. Our service was rated the best, and by 1995, in three years, this start-up, which began its life in one of the suites at the Ramada hotel with me its only employee, had grown to be a significant brand in Sri Lanka.

Telstra had also successfully won a licence to operate a mobile service in West Bengal, partnering with the Modi Group. Telstra had learnt from its experience in Sri Lanka on the importance of speed. The lessons learnt in Sri Lanka were applied to this new Telstra venture in India.

In 1995, the first mobile call was made in India. Chief Minister of West Bengal Jyoti Basu called the Union Communication Minister, Sukh Ram. It was made on the Modi Telstra network.

Modi Telstra, however, was not the first to launch the new digital GSM mobile service in South Asia. That honour was also to an operator in Sri Lanka. We had new competition.

The fourth entrant in this crowded market, Dialog, launched in 1995.

The Maharaja Organisation, a large conglomerate, were awarded another mobile license in Sri Lanka. They subsequently sold the license to Telecom Malaysia. Dr. Hans Wijesuriya was a young engineer just returned from completing his PhD in the UK. He joined that team.

A new digital technology standard called GSM was being rolled out in Europe and had the support of most of the countries there. Dialog adopted this standard. This standard was the game changer in the Industry. As more countries adopted this one standard, the volumes allowed handsets to come down in price. Countries in Asia with large populations, such as India and Indonesia, adopted this standard, and it gathered momentum.

None of us appreciated the impact the GSM would have in Asia or the mobile space, globally. No one envisaged what was to follow and how mobile phones would be an essential accessory to people, like a watch on their wrist.

As an analogue operator, we had to lift our game due to this new threat. We did have the customer base and had captured many premium customers.

We launched a new loyalty programme called Club Magnate. It was a unique programme that had not been done in the communications industry, globally. I had observed the frequent-flyer programmes of airlines and decided to model the loyalty programme on those lines. We went beyond the issue of a loyalty card and accrual of credits depending on the billing of the customer. We pampered the premium customers with gifts and invitations to special events. We sponsored stage plays and concerts and had premium seats reserved for our customers. Club Magnate was a sought after privilege; it had become a status symbol. I would get many calls from customers lobbying me to change their status from a gold card to platinum.

Club rugby was a popular seasonal sport and one that was watched by many of our premium customers. Sponsorships of sports teams by a telecommunications company was rare at that time. We were approached by the CH&FC, a rugby club, for a nominal sponsorship. I met with the chair of the rugby committee, Kishin Butani. We worked out a much bigger deal.

We created many firsts, including a corporate box for VIP guests at the home games, a concept not in existence at that time. We served food and drinks to these VIP guests during the match. Business magazines were not common at that time. *Lanka Monthly Digest*, a new business magazine, was just launched by a good friend, Hiran H. We had played tennis together in our youth. We gave a free subscription of this new publication to our Club Magnate customers. These were the some of the most sought after privileges of the Club Magnate customers. We created a buzz among the premium customers with Club Magnate. We retained our highest-paying customers.

The success of Mobitel was well publicised in Telstra internal communications. Peter Shore had moved on to be managing director of consumer and commercial in the larger, merged Telstra. My son Viruben was twelve years old, and we needed to consider his future in high school. Australia was home. The family came first. It was time to move back.

The year was 1996. Microsoft launched the Windows 95 operating system globally and for the first time enabled easier access to the Internet through Explorer. Bill Gates had correctly predicted the power of the Internet. He had worked with his team to enable the personal computer to easily access the Internet. Larry Page and Sergy Brin, the founders of Google, had met the previous year for the first time at Stanford. That game changer called Google was not yet invented.

In 1996, I decided to return to Sydney and Telstra. I felt we had established a great brand and built a great company. It was hard leaving when you are at the peak, but sometimes that's exactly when you should start something new.

It's with renewal you change; it's with change you grow.

At Mobitel, it was the speed at which we set up the company, built the network around Colombo, the capital of Sri Lanka, and launched the service in a space of a few months that took the competition by surprise. This led to our success. We took risks. Giving the order to Ericsson in Australia to ship the mobile-switching exchange even before we had a license to operate in the country was a risk. As the ship sailed from Australia, we did everything to make sure as it landed we had a place to install the equipment that was the heart of the mobile network.

I had no office space, no staff. In a frantic few months, we had found a new office building that was still being completed. We set up one or two tables in this vast empty space on the third floor. While workmen still worked on finishing the building, we interviewed staff.

My own experience in achieving success, by being faster in serving customer needs, being faster than the competition, led me to form some views about speed and its relationship to success.

I built this theory based on my own experiences that "speed equals success." I subsequently wrote an article, on this theory for *LMD*. The article titled "Speed Can Kill…Your Business" appeared in July 2000.

Since that time, I have refined my thoughts on the subject and have presented the subject to the many teams I have had the pleasure of leading. After taking charge of any job, whether it was as COO in

Aktel in Bangladesh or as CEO of Transcend in Kolkata in India, all the team leaders were given my presentation on "Speed Equals Success." Any book about my life or about passing on the lessons I have learnt will not be complete unless this simple concept is explained.

Whoever we are and wherever we are, we can't help but admit to the notion that life seems to get faster by the year. Before we know it, we are in the month of June and still vividly remember the dawn of the year in January. *Where has the time gone?*

It is not that the world is going around the sun faster. That's happening at the same speed as it has been doing for a million years. The fact is that the human race has always been obsessed with speed. This obsession has led to the fact that any new invention or service that increases the speed of our life is guaranteed success.

The motor car increased our speed of travel compared to the horse and carriage and had a significant impact on our lifestyles. The aeroplane made another leap in speed and shrunk the world; it became possible to cut travel times from weeks and months to hours and, maximum, a day. The change from the telegraph tapping Morse code to the telephone, the change from newspapers to television— they all increased the speed at which we communicated and learnt about events across the globe, shrinking the world even further.

The war in Korea and Vietnam was reported in newspapers, and it took days before people learnt about the details of the war. The war in Iraq was reported live on TV, with embedded journalists in the thick of the action. It's the human race's obsession with speed that demands that this is now the norm. No one will accept another major war being reported by newspapers. Can it get even faster? You bet.

The timeframes between significant events and inventions over time has diminished, fuelled by this obsession with speed.

The human race is hurtling at a speed that packs what we usually did in a week into one day. The success of e-mail is due to the speed at which we can now communicate with each other.

It took forty-one years from the invention of the gasoline-powered motor to the first powered flight. Yet it took only twelve years from the first jet-engine-powered flight to supersonic flight. It took seventy-nine years from the invention of the telephone till the first mainframe computer. It took another twenty-six years to get to the personal computer and then only eight years from there to the Internet. Every significant invention has taken less time than the previous one. We now have the smartphones and the apps that have taken less time to get to market.

I used to get a taxi by dialling a number and waiting for the person on the other end to answer the phone. They would take my details and assign a taxi to me, a process that took over fifteen minutes. Today it's an app on my mobile phone—no need to wait. The app is an instant success because it satisfied the human need for speed.

Even with something as basic as food, speed has a profound effect. In 1955, Ray Kroc started the McDonald's hamburger restaurant chain. The basic concept was to serve food fast. In 2013, the global multinational company has over 35,000 outlets in over 118 countries and continues to grow. Its basic concept is the same globally—to serve food fast.

The global food is not a burger. The burger is not the attraction. Yet it has made it in all these countries. It's not the burger people crave. It is the speed of service and convenience that has made it a success.

The type of food MacDonald's serves has changed as the consumers became more aware of the fat content in burgers. They changed to healthier foods, salads, chicken, but the food was still served fast, food that was ready to go in a short time. The children of today, the adults of tomorrow, take a fast-food outlet over the traditional slow restaurant service, any day. Do they really enjoy the food? Or is it that the gratification of hunger is quick, and that's the overriding factor.

The younger generation, brought up in the environment of this increased speed, have an overwhelming desire to get on with it and get on to more interesting things, like a movie or video games. Fast food has not been restricted to burgers, pizza, or fried chicken. In Asia, traditional food is served fast in shopping malls, food courts, and street stalls, and these have become the places of choice for families eating out.

Three street stalls, all offering traditional cooked food, one has a bigger crowd around it than the others. Once you investigate, inevitably, it is due to the fact that that stall is serving its food faster than the competition. Walking up to the check-in counter of the airline, there are three queues. One is longer than the other two; everyone seems to be joining that longer queue. You then observe that even though it's longer, the agent looks efficient and is clearing the passengers a lot faster while the other two have some issue and the agent is on the phone checking something with the supervisor. Which queue will you join? We are so obsessed with speed, we will make the choice of the longer queue, even though we may have enough time for the flight to depart.

In our lifetimes, we have seen many inventions that have increased the speed of our lives but none as significant as the Internet. When I first wrote the article on speed in 2000, there was no Facebook. There was no Twitter, no WhatsApp. There was no Skype.

All were subsequently launched and were successful because they increased the speed. With Facebook, if you're inclined to share, every one of your friends, wherever they may be in the world, knows instantly what you had for dinner. They even see a picture of the meal.

I wrote then that the Internet or World Wide Web was in its infancy and that the Internet, as it was in the year 2000, was like the Model T Ford car when it first came out. It was slow, with limited features and limited to a small group of people. I said then that the development of the Internet will be a lot faster than the development of the motor car. I still believe we haven't seen the Ferrari of the Internet yet. People will vote in governments and incumbents have been changed on the basis of the promise to provide higher speed Internet to the home. Technology is exponentially developing, and the human thirst for speed is driving the fibre to the home.

In 2012, one-in-three couples that married in the United States met online. In 2008, it was one-in-eight couples. There were 1.2 trillion searches on Google every year in 2012. In 2006, this figure was 230 billion. The concept of a social-networking community connected through the Internet was first proposed in the year 2002.

In 2006, Facebook opened to anyone aged over thirteen who had an e-mail address. It was previously restricted to universities and schools. In two years, it had reached 100-million users and in just six years had reached one billion, one-sixth of the population of the world. The success of Facebook is because of its speed, the speed at which it connects you to the close group of friends and relatives you want to keep in touch with. It instantly reveals to this closed group what you have been up to, it's faster than talking to all of those persons, and it is quicker that writing individually to everyone.

The Internet will continue to define our age and be the biggest agent of change in ours and our children's lifetimes.

Microsoft was established in 1976. Five years later in 1981, IBM introduced the first personal computer, and Bill Gates had convinced them to introduce it with the Windows operating system that he and a few others had developed. In 1995, Bill Gates became the richest man in the world. That's from obscurity to the richest man in the world in nineteen years. Never in history has anyone or any company created wealth so quickly.

Bill Gates success was not due to the fact that he developed an operating system for the PC. In reality the operating system was pretty basic, rudimentary, and had a lot of bugs. He succeeded because he increased the speed at which we could interact with computers. Prior to Windows, the operating system was called DOS, and you needed to be a computer geek to operate any PC. Windows changed that. By being more user friendly and simple, it increased the speed with which you could instruct the computer to perform. This in turn opened the access to ordinary people who did not need to have a computing degree.

There are many more examples of how success came to those who increased the speed. One example is that of Michael Dell, who founded Dell Computers. He changed the speed at which consumers could purchase computers.

Dell Computers were just another PC maker like many others in the market. Most others sold their PCs and laptops in stores. Dell changed the business model to rise above the rest and be successful. Customers could access the Dell website, configure the version of the computer they want, and within two hours, the computer was assembled and shipped out of the door—no computers in inventory,

only parts. He changed the whole business model by completely
bypassing the distributor, shop fronts, and salespeople.

His success ultimately is because he increased the speed at which he
satisfied customers. He also gave complete access to information such
as stock levels, and this information enhanced the speed at which
customers could make decisions, further enhancing the experience
of speed when dealing with Dell as opposed to the competition.

Speed equals success.

Chapter 8

Riding the Asian Wave

In 1996, I returned home. The politics within the Telstra organisation had not abated. The whole point of the merger was to make it an efficient organisation. Staff numbers in the old Telecom Australia exceeded 90,000. Staff cuts were inevitable. Frank Blount, a US senior executive, had been brought in to create one organisation from these two companies. In 1996, a few years after the merger, the staff cuts were happening. Employees from senior management down were concerned about their jobs and watching their backs.

I had left an organisation in 1992 that had a family culture, a close knit and small team. Everyone knew each other. This was OTC. I had returned to a behemoth of an organisation, everyone confused, everyone not sure of their job. There was still a culture of them and us, even four years after the merger.

I had thought a CEO who had blazed a trail by successfully starting up the first mobile operation outside of Australia for Telstra would at least be recognised and given some options of developing himself within the parent organisation. Wrong. No one really cared.

The mobile division did not want to know me. I was not one of them. They were based in Melbourne. My interest too was low in joining them as any job would mean a move from Sydney.

Peter Shore gave me a position with the commercial and consumer division as service improvement project lead for New South Wales. It was meant to be a parking slot while a more challenging operational role became available. After the excitement of running Mobitel, this was a bit like a nail prick to the tyre. I was gently deflating.

Alan L. was the partner at Amrop International, a search firm. Joyce Y. was his colleague. They approached me about a new role in Australian Defence Industries (ADI). ADI was owned by the federal government at that time. ADI operated the naval engineering facility at Garden Island in Sydney harbour. It manufactured weapons and missiles, manufactured the Bushranger armoured vehicle, and had a systems group that did command, control, and communications for naval ships. David R. was the CEO of the systems group of ADI. The company had recently acquired Stanilite Electrical from the receiver. Stanilite, the company, had gone bust. I was a bit apprehensive at first, but the challenge was clear.

The main reason for ADI making the acquisition was that Stanilite had the contract to equip the ANZAC warships with their all their communication equipment. The non-defence, commercial business was an additional headache they did not want but had to take as part of the deal negotiated. They needed someone from outside the defence industry who would know how to salvage this section of the business.

David R. was a really easy person to work with. The office was in North Ryde a short drive from my home. I decided to take the challenge and move from Telstra.

It was a tough move and an easy one, both at the same time. I had joined OTC. They had moved me and my family to Australia from England, and I had worked in the organisation for around eight years, the longest I had worked in any one organisation. I have not worked that long in any organisation since, and I am unlikely to do so again. I had a sense of belonging and loyalty to OTC. They had given me the opportunity to get to the "C" level.

The merger of OTC and Telecom Australia had changed the organisation completely. It was not so much a merger, as TA had around 90,000 staff at that time and OTC around 2,000; it was a complete takeover, and the culture changed. I could not recognise this organisation as OTC anymore. It was tough to leave OTC; it was easier to leave this behemoth.

There were many challenges in this new role at ADI. One was the morale of the team. They had gestated in receivership for some time, many were uncertain of their future, and some of the good people had left. Another challenge was that there were two teams. They were split, one in Sydney and the other in Perth. Not only were they split geographically at two ends of the continent, they were poles apart in what they did. One was an R&D team located in Sydney; the other was a manufacturing facility in Perth. The R&D team were developing a new type of digital radio equipment to a US standard called APCO-25. The Perth team were manufacturing an analogue base station for mobile communications. The main customer was Telstra, purchasing the equipment for its rural network, but the equipment and technology were coming to the end of their lives. Orders were reducing.

The teams, culturally and what they did, could not be more apart.

I enthusiastically took the challenge. I had this team of about 150 people, all hoping I had some magic touch to solve their problems.

I soon found more and more issues as I got deeper into understanding the business. I travelled to Perth many times to get to know the team there. They had a deep mistrust of the HQ in Sydney, and this had been a historical issue even during the time before receivership and the ADI acquisition.

I recruited a new sales team to look at opportunities in Australia and beyond. I also recruited Donna as my executive assistant. I recently asked her to pen some words of her time at ADI and working with me.

> I joined ADI as it was an exciting, evolving time in the telecommunications industry, but more importantly, the role of executive assistant reporting to Vijay was a step up for me in my career at that time.
>
> Working for Vijay for almost two years was an incredible learning experience. He was a wonderful mentor, always patient, and was well respected by his colleagues and staff. A major highlight was Vijay's commitment toward career development for his staff via workshops, leading by example, and sharing his insights on leadership. I can't ever remember a time that Vijay raised his voice to anyone—his demeanour was always cool and calm.
>
> I feel grateful to have worked with Vijay and at ADI. My experience there was instrumental in gaining future executive-assistant roles in large corporations.

David and the senior management team, including me, came to the conclusion after giving it our best shot that the Perth factory had to shut. It was bleeding cash. The Sydney team had a new product that was still a prototype. We decided to focus on productising the APCO-25 base station.

It was a tough call. I joined the human resources team that carried the prepared letters for the staff in Perth, detailing the terms of the redundancy. I decided that I had to be there in person. It was one of the hardest four-hour flights to make. I was mulling over the words and how I would handle the emotions in terminating so many people who I had got to know. I had been on family picnics with them in Perth on some of my previous visits. They were a close-knit team. They had looked up to me. Most of them were aware of the impending terminations, but it was still hard.

In contrast, the Sydney team were not so close, as a unit. They were developing the radio base station that would comply with the new APCO-25 standard. In 1997, there were two new standards for the public mobile radio (PMR). *PMR* is the term used for the two-way radios used by the police, ambulance, and fire services for their communications in the field. One was the European standard called TETRA, and the other was the US standard called APCO-25. These were both the new digital standard for PMR.

There were many manufacturers making the new TETRA-standard radio base station, but only Motorola in the USA and this team here at ADI had a working prototype of the APCO-25-compatible base station.

The lack of funding during the period of receivership had meant there were delays to the development of the product. We put some focus and closed up the spec and took on a deadline to complete the product. The closure of the Perth factory gave the message to the team that management was serious. Steve T. and his team completed the product and had a working unit.

I made several visits to the United States to understand the market and visited trade shows to see the competitors and potential partners. We had a great ally and consultant, Jim C., who was working for us and would get us to meet the right people. We finally licensed the product to other PMR companies in the United States as we realized this was the best model for that market so far away.

It was the summer of 1997. I was in London, UK. I had just arrived from New Delhi in India and was on my way to the USA.

I had several meetings with top military officials in New Delhi and had introduced ADI and the new APCO-25 radio base station product we had. I had used the officials in the Australian high commission working for Austrade to get me the introductions and to open doors. It was a very preliminary visit, exploring the opportunity. It was low key. Before I left New Delhi for London, I had a strange phone call in my hotel room. It was from the resident correspondent of the *Sydney Morning Herald*. I had no idea how he had got my hotel and my room number. He was fishing for the purpose of my visit, and I played it down, not revealing any details.

Feeling jet lag and tired, I was in a deep sleep when someone started banging loudly on the door of the hotel room in London. I jumped out of bed, thinking there was a fire. The hotel was one that had no 24/7 reception. They locked the door at night and had a security guard-cum-receptionist inside. He was standing there, continually banging the door, asking me to wake up. It was about 5:00 a.m.

"You're wanted on the phone, sir. Please pick up the phone," he said. In my deep sleep, I had not heard the phone ringing by the bed. He put through the call again, and I answered.

It was a very senior executive of ADI on the line. We hardly had any contact with him back in Sydney. It was extremely unusual to have a call from him, particularly at this time in the morning. He was furious. I had no idea why.

After he had calmed down, I got to know that an article had appeared in the *Sydney Morning Herald* that day, stating that ADI was looking to do business in India. ADI kept a low profile, and any press was a no, India having been through several wars with Pakistan. ADI, which also sold missiles and weapons, did not want any association or perception in the media that it was doing business in India.

I had figured out later that the information had leaked from the Austrade office that I was there to the correspondent of the *SMH*. They had also given the details of where I was staying to the reporter. The reporter had made a story out of the most innocuous of information. I guess he was earning his wages, but he had put me in mighty trouble. I later gave my own piece of mind to the Austrade officials in Delhi.

It was 1998. The Asian financial crisis that started in 1997 had taken its toll. The worst-affected countries were Thailand and Indonesia. After riots and protests about the increase in prices of essentials in Indonesia, the leader of thirty years, President Suharto, had to step down. One of the people affected by that crisis in Indonesia was Putera Sampoerna.

Today, Putera is one of the richest Indonesians, valued at over USD 2 billion. Putera's father arrived in Indonesia from China and adopted the Indonesian name *Sampoerna*, which means "perfection." He started mixing cloves with tobacco and hand-wrapping cigarettes called "kreteks," which became very popular in Indonesia. Putera took the business to another level, building factories and becoming the largest tobacco company in Indonesia. His business was acquired by Phillip Morris in 2005.

In 1996, just before the Asian financial crisis, the Sampoerna Group had invested in Transmarco, a listed company in Singapore. Transmarco in turn had invested in a new fixed-wireless license in Sri Lanka. Transmarco was joined by a number of high net-worth individuals in applying and getting the license.

In January, 1996, a truck containing about 400 pounds of explosives crashed through the main gates of the central bank in the city centre of Colombo in Sri Lanka. This was one of the most daring and worst attacks of the LTTE in the heart of Colombo. As gunmen traded fire with security guards, the suicide bomber in the lorry detonated the massive bomb, which tore through the bank and damaged eight other buildings nearby. The lorry was followed by a three-wheeler, or "tuk-tuk," carrying two LTTE cadres armed with automatic rifles and an RPG launcher.

The blast killed at least ninety-one people and injured 1,400 others. At least 100 people lost their eyesight. Among the wounded were two US citizens, six Japanese, and one Dutch national. One of those US citizens was one of the investors in Lanka Bell.

In spite of the injuries sustained while being in the Hilton Hotel, this individual continued his efforts to start up Lanka Bell.

In 1998, after two years of investment and when the financial crisis hit, the business needed a new strategy. As a start-up, it had sucked a lot of cash.

While still working at ADI, I received a call from Singapore; a boutique headhunter was keen to meet with me. He arranged for me to visit Singapore, and I met with one of the investors. I was offered the position of managing director/CEO of Lanka Bell.

It was an agonising decision. I could not take the family. They had returned three years earlier from Sri Lanka and had now settled into schools in Sydney. It would be unfair to uproot them again. The offer was lucrative, and my reputation in Sri Lanka was still strong after my success in Mobitel. The director who interviewed me had outlined the difficulties in the business and the restructuring that had to take place. I relished the challenge.

I did not realize it then, but as I reflect on my career, this was a pivotal moment. Although calling Australia home, I was making a choice to ride the Asia wave. The wave that gathered momentum with the opening up of the mobile sector in India and Bangladesh, the Asian tigers that bounced back from the financial crisis to register record growth, year on year.

Australia, in spite of its vast expanse and small population, missed out creating a vibrant and competitive telecommunications industry that could have created many more jobs.

A cabinet battle and decision in 1990 forever changed the landscape of telecommunication in Australia. The price Australian consumers pay for their calls and for data today is around three times what consumers pay in Asia. The technology is the same; the rates are three times cheaper because of vibrant competition, multiple players, and no dominance of a single player.

Bernard Keane relates the event in February 1990:

> "This is a fucking second-rate decision from a second-rate government."

> That was Paul Keating, storming out of the Hawke cabinet in September 1990, after it had approved Kim Beazley's proposal to merge Telecom and OTC and have a managed duopoly in telecommunications.

Keating had wanted OTC to stay separate and become the basis for a competitor to Telecom, and open competition. Instead, the debt-laden Aussat got that role.

The issue, and the fight between Beazley and Keating, dominated politics after the 1990 election. Keating's fury was partly derived from the growing leadership tensions with Hawke, who sided with Beazley (there was by that stage talk that Hawke was promoting Beazley to replace him rather than Keating), but was mostly genuine. Beazley's plan was cooked up in concert with Telecom management and, critically, Telecom's unions — this was the days when Telecom had nearly 90,000 workers.

Beazley was terrified of upsetting the powerful public sector unions. Keating pushed the Treasury line for more competition and giving a serious competitor a leg-up to take on the established giant. He lost. The best place to read about the clash is Mark Westfield's ripping yarn of a media policy history, *The Gatekeepers*.

Telstra was thus born in the conflict between politics and economic theory, and has remained there ever since.

We cannot predict what would have happened if the decision was reversed and the basis of competition in the Australian market was made by setting up Telecom Australia against OTC.

My view may be biased. However, I still strongly believe the decision was the wrong one. What was set up was the dominance of the market by one player, and subsequent players from overseas—such as Cable and Wireless of UK, SingTel of Singapore, and Vodafone of UK, large as they may be in their own markets—had no chance ever of breaking this dominance, the dominance of Telstra.

The decision was wrong because OTC was a vibrant and cash-rich organisation with dominance in the international communications in and out of Australia. Telecom Australia (TA) would have had to set up new infrastructure facilities and arrange corresponding agreements with all countries around the world. This would have given time for OTC to set up its local network and distribution within Australia. OTC already had local presence as it had international exchanges in all the major cities. More importantly, OTC had a relationship with all Australian telecom users, who were using them for their international calls. It had local brand presence.

Aussat, on the other hand, was a debt-ridden satellite organisation. It had very limited access to the Australian consumer. The new investor was given a license and had to buy the company with its debt. It was akin to giving Telstra the pole position in the race. Aussat had no local brand presence.

Telstra raced to the front, and no one ever came close. Telstra strangled every competitor with denials to access their last-mile network. The Howard government had another opportunity to put things right before the privatisation in 1997. They were urged to split the behemoth into the retail arm and a network wholesale arm. The short-term greed to get the maximum price for Telstra in that float ensured Telstra stayed as-is.

OTC would have been a much more credible competitor, would have had the local knowledge and expertise, and would have been a better partner for an overseas investor. Today, Optus is a very weak niche player, and the biggest loser is the Australian consumer as they pay three times the rates for data paid by consumers in Asia.

For me personally, it meant that the opportunities were elsewhere.

It was like sitting on the beach with a surfboard by your side. The view was great, the beach welcoming, but the sea was calm. Asia, on the other hand, was embracing competition. There was no dominant player. The boom in China was fuelling growth everywhere. There were waves just forming and working themselves to a crescendo. I wanted to be involved and part of that action. I wanted to ride the Asian wave.

Lanka Bell was certainly like riding a wave, in a very stormy sea.

They say that the values of an organisation are like the soul of a person. Lanka Bell had no values. The culture was toxic. The company had a contract with one of the Bell companies to provide around thirty experts to advise the company and start operations. A year after the operations had started, they were still there. It was not in their interest to localize the operations; many of them were comfortably holed up at the Mount Lavinia Hotel along the coast south of Colombo and were enjoying life and the pleasures that could be purchased.

The initial team had spent money—on land acquisition, large warehouses, and materials way above the market rate and what other telecom operators were paying locally. They were comparing costs to what they would pay in the USA. They had contended they were getting a good deal.

Once the cash stopped, Lanka Bell was struggling with these huge costs.

I gave the board some confidence that we could localize the operations and cut costs, and we terminated that manpower contract with the US Bell company. I later found that some of those so-called experts were doing very menial jobs in the United States.

Slowly, with the management team I had, we set our standards higher and brought in new members and got rid of some staff who were hired by these so-called experts for the wrong reasons. Others we could turn around just by providing some leadership and setting standards of behaviour that were expected.

People react to the leader's behaviour. Those leaders who don't walk the talk, espouse high values and ethics, and don't practice that themselves cannot expect to have a fully motivated and engaged team.

Sunil L. was very familiar with the way I worked as he had been in Mobitel, and he held the senior position in sales and marketing in both organisations. I was glad he was already in the company when I joined. Sales and marketing were the least of my worries. He was able to give me very valuable advice.

Gamini W. was a senior finance management executive recruited from John Keels and was CFO of Lanka Bell. I soon worked out that he was a person with a high set of values and ethics but was quiet in voicing his views unless pushed. I gave him the freedom to voice his views and discovered much from those interactions. We gradually built trust and a team at the senior management level and united to attack the market and build a business.

I needed someone I could trust as my PA in this hostile environment, and I approached Natali, my former PA at Mobitel to join.

There was a high degree of resistance to change in the company. Right through the ranks, they had all got comfortable in an organisation without values.

Gradually we turned it around.

In less than two years, we had become profitable and cash positive. We were able to service some of the large debt we had inherited, but essentially, operationally the business was profitable.

I recently asked Natali again to pen some thoughts of her time working for me at Lanka Bell, just to get someone else's perspective.

> I left Mobitel in December 1998 to work as Vijay's PA at Lanka Bell in January 1999.
>
> The period at Lanka Bell was different to Mobitel because Vijay was on a different mission. He had to restructure the company, unlike a start-up, which was so much easier. Lanka Bell was restructured and revamped within a span of one year. The task at hand for me was to follow-up with Vijay's direct reports, the GMs. It was no easy task, but Vijay had his full confidence in me, and I managed the work and tasks entrusted without much hassle.
>
> He introduced the balanced score card, which was new to Colombo at that time, and also introduced the Year-End Gala Staff Dance. Vijay also kept the team spirit on a high note by organizing many staff-related events and awards programs which boosted the morale of the staff.
>
> The many training programs he conducted were a highlight. We used to look forward to these programmes.
>
> Vijay's strength was that he respected and managed people so well. He knew exactly how to get the best out of all of us. He also believed that one should earn respect and not demand for it.

I consider it a privilege to have worked as personal assistant to Vijay Watson on two occasions. Both organizations are listed on the stock exchange of Colombo and has given employment to thousands of men and women from all walks of life in Sri Lanka. The knowledge and exposure I gained by working for Vijay Watson is immeasurable. Thank you, Vijay, for the confidence you placed in me.

David at ADI had introduced me to the balanced score card. It was based on a simple concept. The fundamental theme of BSC is that "if you can't measure it, you can't manage it." The key is to find the right measures, the measures that drive that particular business. I used the BSC to drive change and profitability in Lanka Bell.

I read and understood the Kaplan and Norton book. I developed training material and conducted training with the leadership team and all key managers. I did not employ consultants. I conducted the course myself. This made a big difference to its adaptation by the team.

Managers know the details; they know what they have to measure. My job was to coach them on the concept and to let them work out the right measures.

In 1999, it was expensive to buy ERP systems like SAP. They were still running on the mainframe computers. The capture of real-time data from a business was still a dream. Data is stored in various sources—in the accounting system, in staff computers, in call centres. During that time, important data was also not captured. Every time a customer would call the company—to make a query or to complain—the call contains valuable data. It contains data on the business and how it is performing. Unless this data is captured, analysed, and summarised, it is really difficult to know how a business is performing.

Traditional measurements were always financial. However, this information was always historical. It told you the results after the event. The balanced part of the BSC tells us we need to look beyond the financials.

Current ERP systems and business intelligence systems are giving managers much more visibility in real time about their business.

My role in Edotco is also about introducing the key tools to enable visibility of part of the business that had no visibility before. A few years ago, I wrote an article in the *LMD* about the importance of having real time information to make critical decisions in managing the business. The article was as follows:

> The aircraft doors were shut. Sitting comfortably and watching the safety video were 433 passengers and twenty-six crew members. The Airbus A380 aircraft was barely two years old and was the first to be delivered to Qantas, the Australian airline. It was 9.30 a.m. on the fourth of November 2010, and they were being pushed back from the gate at Changi Airport in Singapore, a routine flight from Singapore to Sydney. QF 32 taxied to the runway.
>
> Unusually, this morning, there were five pilots on board the flight. There was the captain of the flight, Richard de Crespigny, the first and second officer. This would normally make up the full complement of the flight crew for the A380. However, in addition, on this day, there were two more captains on the flight. The first, a captain who was being trained as a check captain and the second the supervisor

training him, an experienced check captain. There were over 72,000 years flying experience in the cockpit that day.

The A380 was powered by four Rolls Royce Trent 900 engines. Within ten minutes of the plane lifting off the ground, the passengers heard a loud bang. The left side engine nearest the cabin had exploded. Shrapnel from the exploding engine had punctured part of the wing and damaged the fuel system causing leaks. Damage was also done to one hydraulic system and the anti-lock brakes. The other engines went into degraded mode.

Debris from the exploding aircraft engine fell on the Indonesian island of Bantam. Large chunks just missed a school but caused no injuries on the ground.

On seeing the debris, which included chunks that had part of the red, flying-kangaroo logo, news was passed by mobile phone to friends in China that a Qantas plane had crashed. This news, picked up by the newswire services, spread back to Australia, and the Qantas share price started falling. Alan Joyce, the CEO of Qantas, was driving back to work from a meeting when he noticed the shares of Qantas plunging by 5 percent for no apparent reason. He quickly rang his office to be told that the first of its fleet of six A380s, the pride of the airline, was still flying but had a catastrophic engine failure and was limping back to Singapore.

The cockpit was lit up with fifty-four alarms. More critically, there were twelve system errors that had to be dealt with immediately. It's hard to imagine how the crew reacted in the cockpit at that time, but the results demonstrated some extraordinary leadership and management of the situation. Having assessed that the plane was controllable, Captain de Crespigny made the decision to land back at Changi and flew the plane while the other four members dealt with the system errors and alarms. Not having this particular situation simulated in their training made every move risky, but the training, collective brain power, the discipline of leadership, and taking responsibility allowed them to work in this confined space as equals, to resolve the problems at hand.

As they came in to land, fuel was leaking from the left wing, communication channels were not usable, and one VHF channel was being used to link the cockpit to the emergency crew now standing in wait back at Changi Airport. The mobile phone was used to contact the control tower and Qantas ground staff and alert them of the situation. The plane landed using its maximum braking load due to its weight on landing, and four tyres burst. The braking raised the temperature of the wheels to 900 degrees centigrade, and fuel continued leaking as the plane came to rest. To add to this inflammable situation, one of the engines could not be shut down. The passengers, however, walked off the plane, without anyone being injured.

The passengers would later remark how they were given constant messages from Captain de Crespigny through the flight, reassuring them throughout the ordeal. No one realized how close they had come to disaster.

In business, too, we have many such situations, a sudden unexpected event where we need to immediately take responsibility, throw hierarchy out of the window, all levels of managers working together to solve the problem at hand. While there may be one manager ultimately responsible, it is those organizations with the right leadership and culture where all the experienced people would chip in, know what to do to prioritize and systematically deal with the issue while the business is still operational and the customers assured and kept loyal to the brand. An essential ingredient for success is to have an effective scorecard that is measuring all parts of the business, like the panel on the cockpit of the A380 aircraft. Without these indicators, one is figuratively flying blind.

Unfortunately, most companies don't have scorecards that can alert them sufficiently when such disasters strike.

National Australia Bank (NAB) customers, in the same month as the Qantas incident on the twenty-fifth of November 2010, found that they could not withdraw money from the ATM. Payments and loans were not credited and debited. The incident dragged on for five days as the bank struggled to contain the effects of a software glitch. Communication was late and confusing. No one could tell when the

issue would be resolved. This is in stark contrast to
the way the pilots resolved the issue on Qantas 32.

One major difference was the ability to see in real
time the consequences of an incident such as the
explosion in the engine or the software glitch. A
progressive business today will have more than the
balanced scorecard that was proposed by Kaplan
and Norton in the '90s. It will have a scorecard
that would be very similar to the control panel of a
modern aircraft, a scorecard that would be scanning
in real time all the information of the business
analysing and presenting it in a dashboard visual
display. The rest is then leadership and management
of the situation.

I had worked for many supportive boards. Keeping them informed
at formal board meetings was enough. They understood what I was
doing in the business, and they had their own methods of getting
feedback from the market and from staff to make a judgement about
my performance.

Some other boards are different. You need to also develop personal
relationships with the directors outside of the formal meetings. I had
not done this very well at LB.

I was on leave with the family, having a holiday in Malaysia. I had
travelled from Sri Lanka; they had travelled from Australia. Towards
the end of the holiday, I got a call saying that one of the directors
wanted to meet me in Singapore. I was asked to stop by on my
way back from Kuala Lumpur. I met him in the hotel, completely
unaware of the agenda. He informed me that the board had lost its
confidence in me and that he wanted me to resign but continue to

serve my three-months' notice while they found a new MD. I was in shock.

The job had taken its toll. I was also contemplating leaving soon. But, the timing had to be mine.

I had rescued this company from certain bankruptcy. I had felt good that things had turned around. I had felt wrongly that the board was supportive. I knew I had also made some enemies.

There were no new investments from the shareholders, and we had to manage with the cash we were collecting from the business. I had left my family in Australia to manage this business and give it a platform for growth. I was hurt. I kept my emotions in check. I said, "Fine. Are all directors in agreement with this decision?" He just mentioned that it was a decision of the board.

The politics among the board was quite intense and active; it was hard to know what went on behind the scenes. I was convinced this was not a unanimous decision. The board consisted of representatives of a number of shareholders including Nortel, the Canadian company. Nortel had provided all the equipment and had offered a credit line and hence had a seat on the board. A new investor, the Japanese venture capital firm AIDEC, had recently invested, and they also had a seat on the board. They were all based in Singapore. I asked for some time. As this was sudden, I had to reflect on what the director had said. He insisted we meet again in the evening and I sign the letter of resignation.

I was highly stressed. I had not expected this. I needed to compose myself and get this sorted. I needed to hear from the other directors myself. I immediately got in touch with the director who was representing Nortel and said I wanted to meet him. He gave me an appointment, and I saw him that day. Similarly, I went to meet the principals of AIDEC.

Once I had explained my position, my achievements to date, and the challenges facing the company in the next few months, including the Y2K issue, they gave me their full support and asked me to leave the matter to them. The meeting in the evening with the director who had given me this devastating news was cancelled. I breathed a sigh of relief; I had bought some time.

I continued as the MD and CEO, but my mind was made up. I would leave as soon as I felt I had sorted outstanding issues. I wanted to leave on my terms.

I often reflect on how that situation arose. I felt I had given my all in the job, and yet the board had been not been fully informed and were not aware of my effort. I had presented many times to the board the progress and the achievements. My problem was my communication and the building of the relationship with the directors of the board outside the formal meeting. I had not followed up and developed individual relationships with the directors of the board. I had allowed others to influence them. I learnt a valuable lesson, how important it is to manage up as it is to manage down. My nature, my natural instincts, were to get on with the job and that results were everything. In reality, the results count for far less; the relationships count for much more.

Y2K was a serious problem. Most programmes and computers used two digits for the date. So 1998 would be 98. When the year 2000 occurred, they would record 00, and the computer would interpret this as 1900. In addition, the year 2000 was a leap year. We were particularly concerned about the billing system, which used dates for their calculations. We prepared and fixed the Y2K potential problem. It was a tense time as the clock struck midnight on the December 31. *Had we fixed all the billing and accounting software issues?* We had a delayed celebration for the new year, after we were convinced most of the issues were fixed.

In March 2000, the dot-com bubble burst. Around $5 trillion was wiped out of the value of companies on the stock market. The signs of an impending crisis were written everywhere, but no one seemed to be taking notice. People were setting up companies that made no business sense but had a dot-com on the end of their name, and there were people queuing to fund those companies. A good example of the mood at that time was Kozmo.com.

The average age of the founders was in the early twenties. Kozmo.com took orders over the Internet and promised one-hour delivery of a wide range of products, including an entire evening's complement of food and videos, with no delivery fee and at a price roughly equal to what one would pay at retail. As it turned out, the business model was really selling $10 bills for $5. But Kozmo.com also got its money (including $60 million from Amazon) and managed to run through $250 million of venture capital before shutting its doors just fourteen months later.

The first signs of trouble came from the companies themselves. Many reported huge losses, and some folded outright within months of their offering. "Siliconaires" were moving out of $4 million estates and back to the room above their parents' garage.

In the year 1999, there were 457 IPOs, most of which were Internet- and technology-related. Of those 457 IPOs, 117 doubled in price on the first day of trading. In 2001, the number of IPOs dwindled to 76, and none of them doubled on the first day of trading.

I decided to return to Sydney, Australia, in the year 2000.

I spent the next few years in Sydney. I had been away travelling and living overseas. My family had been in Sydney. I was forty-five years old. I needed to just spend time with them. The children were both at a critical juncture in their educations. The two years at Lanka

Bell had taken their toll on me and my motivation. I needed time to recharge.

It was around this time that, encouraged by the dot-com boom, I set up my own company called Lanka Link. This was a real business but before its time. I had identified that the diaspora of Sri Lankans living abroad had a need from time to time of services they would like to have delivered in Sri Lanka. For example, a son living in Australia may want to gift his mother who lived in Sri Lanka on her birthday by having delivery of a cake or some flowers. I set up the website and also had one of the early payment gateways to accept credit cards. This was early in the dot-com era, and the mainstream public were not confident of using credit cards on the Internet. After a couple of years, I closed the business.

A couple of years later, a site called Kapruka.com was set up to provide this service. It is an extremely successful business and has won many awards. The business employs over 200 people and has shop fronts and its own delivery vehicles.

It was not meant to be, for me.

I joined a NASDAQ-listed company called Airspan. They were happy for me to be based in Sydney, and I travelled the Asia region setting up their service centres and a customer-support network.

In 2001, we were all confronted with the 9/11 terrorist attack, and the bombings and uncertainty that we had endured while living in Sri Lanka suddenly was mainstream; the world and its innocence changed.

By 2004, the children had completed two milestones. Our son Viruben had passed out from university. He was about to start working. Naomi, our daughter, had just started university.

My wife and I could, if we wanted to, return to Asia. After a four-year break in Sydney, I was observing that Asia was buzzing yet again. The growth and excitement of new challenges were alluring.

I decided to surf once more.

Chapter 9

Surfing the Largest Wave

It was 2004. I had arrived at a juncture in my life where I needed to take stock. My motivation and passion to lead change had returned. I was turning fifty the next year. The world had bounced back from the dot-com bust. The telecommunications industry in Australia was still ordinary; the dominance of Telstra just killed any real competition.

South Korea had just passed 71 percent of their households subscribing to the broadband Internet service, up from 1 percent in 1995. It is the most Internet-wired nation in the world. The economies in Asia had grown 6.3 percent the previous year, making it the most dynamic region in the world.

After a time, exploring opportunities that were available in Asia, I started discussions with key people in Telecom Malaysia International (TMI). I was offered a position as the chief operating officer (COO) in Aktel in Bangladesh.

At that time, I did not know much about Bangladesh. I was curious why many of the Malaysians were not so keen on this posting. It was a relatively easy discussion with TMI; there were not many other contenders for the post.

Telecom Malaysia had set up an international arm to invest in telecom networks overseas. Much like OTC International in Australia, TMI had been extremely successful in Sri Lanka with their investment in Dialog. They had a market leadership position there. TMI had a mobile license in Bangladesh and was providing the service under the brand Aktel.

The operations in Bangladesh that were done in conjunction with a local partner were not doing so well. They had a very weak number-two position in a three-player mobile market. Grameen Phone was the market leader. The other company was Citycell, owned by Singapore Telecom. A new, fresh investment was being made by TMI to expand the mobile-network coverage and strengthen the business in the face of a new threat. Licenses were to be issued to Warid and Oraascom, two companies from the Middle East, flush with cash. The competition was about to get fierce. Aktel had to strengthen its position in the market before the competition entered the fray.

Nothing in my life experiences prepared me for the shock of Dhaka.

I had never, ever seen so many people in one place in my life. My brain could not compute the crowds. I was in shock at the poverty, the squalor I was witnessing. Every bit of greenery was covered in a light layer of dust. I could not get used to how close people could get to you; your sense of personal space was compromised. I had not experienced this human volume in any of the countries I had lived in before. It was a confronting experience, one I never got used to.

As the Malaysian Airlines plane descended to land, I observed a very flat land with multiple lakes filled with brackish water. Some were small ponds; some were large lakes. The buildings were short. Four- to five-storied, flat-roof structures, so close to each other, it was like a farm of buildings. It did not seem too bad from the air.

The airport was one of the worst I had seen in the region at that time. The long queues at immigration started to warm you to this notion that you were in one of the most densely populated cities in the world.

Once you got out of immigration and saw the crowds staring at you from behind the barriers, you knew you were in some place where god decided to rain people. The noise, the raising of the voice between people who, when you observed, were having a normal conversation. I had been used to populations of 21 million people in Australia, the continent, and in Sri Lanka, the country. But I had not witnessed that population in one city before.

To this day, I am amazed that this city runs without daily fights and anarchy. I have been caught in the midst of one of their *hartals*. These are political strikes called by the opposition political party, demanding all establishments join in sympathy to their cause. I have seen the violent crowds, how they will turn on anything. Whipped into a frenzy, they will destroy and kill.

Yet daily life is somehow undertaken with a lot of patience and give-and-take.

I got to know the Bangladeshis as very emotional people but also very tolerant, extremely patriotic, and proud of being Bangladeshi. I came to appreciate their enthusiasm, their excitement at the smallest of things. They warmed to praise and encouragement more than any other teams I had led. They sapped knowledge as long as you would share and were sincere. You had to walk the talk.

Aktel was the brand of the mobile service in Bangladesh owned and operated by TMI and a local partner, the AK Khan group. Aktel was a play on words. Combining the initials of the local partner AK, but also "AK" meant one in Bangla.

The AK Khan group was founded just after the end of World War II while the country was still part of India. The founder started his business in Chittagong, which was a thriving port city under the British. Mr. A.K. Khan held positions in the British-ruled India legislature and was uniquely also a minister in the Pakistan government when the country was East Pakistan after partition.

His son, Zahiruddin Khan, was the chairman of Aktel when I arrived in Dhaka to take over as COO. Zahiruddin Khan had also been a minister in the Bangladesh government as minister for planning and minister for industry from 1991 to 1995.

My responsibilities as COO was for all of the business except Finance. The chief financial officer (CFO) was Rajadurai Selvadurai, a Malaysian from TMI. He and I reported to the managing director, Nasir Bin Baharom.

The MD of the TMI group was Christian De Faria, who was a French national and spoke English with a strong French accent. He was on the board. Dr. Hans Wijesuriya, the MD from the Dialog operation in Sri Lanka, was also on the board of Aktel. In them, I had two allies to make the changes necessary to prepare and consolidate Aktel in the market before the new competition.

Christian was succeeded by Datuk Yusof Annuar Yaacob who was equally supportive. The TM head was Dato Sri Abdul Wahid Omar who visited Dhaka giving me the privilege of showing him the progress we had made with the business.

I worked out quite early that the local partner had a grip of the business and much more control than was warranted by their shareholding. TMI, not being present in the country and only occasionally attending meetings, had not been paying too much attention to this business. However, the situation in the market was about to change. Unless Aktel changed, it would lose its position to the new players about to enter the market.

We mapped out about seventy-five key projects, and I started to scout the company for the talent I needed to execute on these projects. I selected some young talent in the ranks. I broadcast a search for new talent inside the company and personally interviewed candidates to make up this special pool.

A young, bright manager in Dialog, Supun Weerasinghe, came from time to time to assist me with the projects. Little would he know at that time that ten years later he would be CEO of Robi. Aktel rebranded itself and became Robi in 2010. Supun became CEO in 2014.

I conducted many training programmes for this special pool. I taught them that speed equals success. I now had my army of change agents.

It was the only way to break the entrenched apathy of the existing management team. They were all comfortable in their positions; they would not support the change at the pace I wanted. I was also not aware of who were the moles planted by the local partner. I suspected that there were quite a few of them in the organisation.

There were a few Malaysians I could trust who had been put into key positions. One was Jose Ravi. He was in charge of sales and marketing. The engineering and operations head was Haji Omar Said. Nasir as MD was extremely supportive. He handled the local partner, and we played the good-cop/bad-cop roles.

As a team, we went on a recruitment spree. We quickly built on the existing manpower, opening customer centres and expanding the coverage beyond the confines of Dhaka and Chittagong where Aktel was present at that time. I moved fast. The local partner kept wanting to influence the selection process. I instilled a transparent process and insisted it had to be followed. I was personally involved in any new team recruitment. It was key, getting the right people into the organisation.

The success of our job was in the numbers. When I joined we had around 900,000 customers on our mobile network. When I left two years later, we had increased that to 3 million.

We had expanded in one of the fastest building sprees in my career at that time. We were expanding exponentially, with new sites providing coverage and mobile communication service to new areas daily. Three contractors, Ericsson, Huawei, and Alcatel, were all working night and day. We increased the distribution of SIM cards around the country, opened showrooms and customer centres, and expanded the call centre to handle the volume of calls.

The distribution of the SIM cards was the most intense battle internally. We prevailed with some compromise.

It was a great experience, knowing you were bringing mobile communication to the rural areas of Bangladesh, changing lives and transforming their future. The potential was huge, with a country of 150 million people. I was always keen to attend every opening of our centres around the country. We recruited and gave many jobs, jobs people desperately needed to help their extended families. We built a new brand. We rebranded the company, new logo and new colours, and launched full-page advertisements with new packages taking the battle to Grameen Phone.

In 2005, we were riding the start of this huge wave. We had given Aktel then, Robi now its best shot at facing the new competition from Warid and Banglalink. The wave grew. By end of 2013, the number of mobile connections in the country had surpassed 100 million.

People I had led then comment even today on my style of leadership and how it encouraged them to excel. I never sought to be some particular type of leader; I was taking it day by day, reacting to situations as they presented themselves. I had to be aware of not getting dragged into the details and not micromanaging people. There is a distinction between coaching and mentoring and micromanaging. Many leaders don't get that difference. They get impatient and end up micromanaging rather than stepping back. My passion was to develop people who wanted to improve. I spent a lot of time coaching and training.

I modelled my management style to that of a football manager.

I am not an avid football fan. I did however attend football matches at Old Trafford to watch Manchester United at home during my time studying at university. I was living in Salford near the large city of Manchester, which was not far from Old Trafford. The mid-seventies was a time of economic hardships for the families in Salford and the surrounding areas. Football was a great escape.

As I moved into senior management, I was conscious on the style of leadership that I had to adopt to motivate staff and get results. I began to observe various styles of management, and the role of the football manager fascinated me. It inspired me.

I could imagine the frustration and anxiety of the manager sitting far away from the action, not allowed on to the field and yet totally responsible for the outcome.

As I observed this unique style of management, I became more convinced there were lessons to be learnt. I even wrote about this in one of my articles on leadership later.

The manager of a football team takes full blame if the team loses and all the praise if it wins. He faces the media after the match.

Yet he never kicks a ball in the game and is not allowed on the turf. In football, the manager plans the strategy, does the player acquisitions, coaches the team in particular skills, and then lets the captain and the ten players, who all have specific roles in the field, to get on with it. After the match, he fronts the media. He takes full responsibility.

Sir Alex Ferguson was the manager at Manchester United, and he had been at the helm of the club since 1986. In over thirty-six years, he has won all the possible titles for the club and is rightly credited with the success the club has enjoyed. Although his title may be manager, he is regarded as an exceptional leader.

The manager in football sitting in the stands has a unique view of how the game and the opposition are playing; he can change strategy at the half-time if that is required. At half-time, he has the opportunity to talk and motivate the team. One famous pep talk given by Sir Alex Ferguson during a half-time at a European Cup Final: "At the end of this game, the European Cup will be only six feet away from you, and you'll not even able to touch it if we lose. And for many of you that will be the closest you will ever get. Don't you dare come back in here without giving your all."

Can corporate leaders learn from how teams are managed in football?

We often hear the term *micromanagers* in reference to some corporate leaders who tend to get involved in detail and take decisions that should rightfully be the decisions taken by the team. They are involved to such an extent in daily, mundane, operational matters that there is a fear of making decisions and taking ownership by the rest of the team.

It's as if the manager of the football team is screaming on the field, running with the ball and shouting instructions. The players become less reliant on their own skills and their own reading of the game;

they just pass to whoever the manager is screaming they pass to. No one is looking at the bigger picture, no one is observing the opposition, and the motivation speech at half-time becomes a very operational one where the blame game is played by the manager. Since all he has seen is the action on the field by individuals, he will be drawn to asking individuals why they did this and that. This tends to demotivate individuals and the team. No one is giving the pep talk about the ultimate goal.

The key place where the manager interacts is in the training field. Here he has individual chats with players; he corrects fundamental flaws in technique or attitude. He motivates the player. The team practice particular moves, in defence, in attack.

The manager sets the culture in the team. He motivates, but he lets the team do the work on the field.

Micromanagers in a corporate environment are not leaders. Leaders tell people what to do, not how to do it.

One of the most successful companies this century has been Google. It is on *Fortune's* "Most Admired Companies" list in the top five for many years.

The company was started in the mid-'90s by Sergey Brin and Larry Page. Both engineering students of IT at Stanford, they developed what is now the search engine of choice for most of the world. After six years, they brought in Eric Schmidt as CEO, and both the founders moved to operational roles.

This was the smartest decision made by them.

It is unlikely that the founders of Google, had they continued as the leaders, would have had the discipline and will to resist micromanaging their start-up company. By bringing in a manager like Eric who was able to sit in the stands like a football manager and observe the market and opposition; direct the strategy and acquisitions; and set the culture of the organisation, Google rose from silicon start-up of 200 people in 2001 to its current is position as a global company with 10,000 employees. Google has grown from start-up and ground zero to be 162 on the *Fortune* "Global 500" with revenues of USD 60 billion in 2014.

Eric was another born in 1955.

He graduated with a PhD in IT from the University of California in 1982. He was CEO of Novell before joining Google in 2001. "Google is run by its culture and not by me…we operate under the assumption that everyone including me is extremely dispensable, because ultimately Google is bigger than the individuals who make it," he said in response to a question about his leadership style to the *Washington Post.*

In 2011, Eric Schmidt handed back the reins to Larry Page, one of the founders. The foundations had been built; the culture had been established.

Theodore Roosevelt once said, "The best executive is the one who has sense enough to pick the good men to get what he wants done, and self-restraint enough to keep from meddling with them while they do it."

I had enjoyed riding this wave in Bangladesh. I was ready for a bigger challenge, an even bigger wave.

The biggest wave was happening next door. It was happening in India.

Nokia, the company, started its life as a paper mill on the banks of the Nokianvirta River in Finland. I had come across the company when I was in Mobitel in the early '90s. The company rode the wave of the GSM revolution, which reduced the prices of handsets and made the devices affordable to the mass market. It lead the innovation, and its menu-driven operating system on the phone was the best on the market. By 1998, it was the world leader in mobile phones, a position it grew to in a short span of about eight years. By 2005, it was a global, iconic brand.

In addition to the mobile phones, Nokia also made the switches and the base stations that were part of the mobile network that allowed you to make and receive mobile calls wherever you were. They had built a large market share globally in this area of the business and had a dominant position in India.

India's was one of the fastest growing markets in mobiles and in building the infrastructure to expand its reach to the rural areas of this vast country. The wave had just begun.

In 2005, there were 90 million users of mobile phones in India. By 2013, in just eight years, that was to increase to 752 million ranking it second in the world, having the largest number of mobile users after China.

I wanted to be part of this biggest wave. I had reached the milestone age of fifty. Globally, after China, this was the largest mobile market in the world, and it was about to explode in growth. If I was given the opportunity, I wanted to do this.

Always watch what you wish for.

A head-hunter from Singapore approached me in 2005, Nokia were looking for a new head of services to be based in Gurgaon, close to New Delhi. I decided to take the challenge.

Nothing I had done before prepared me for this challenge.

It was the sheer numbers—one billion people, one huge country, each of them with the competitive nature that was instinct. You had to be competitive in this country if you wanted to be noticed. Everyone had to struggle to get into the limited places in schools, on the bus, on the train.

In 2006, my wife and I moved from Dhaka to Gurgaon. It was a satellite city of New Delhi, a new city, all new buildings, full of call centres and other high-tech companies. Gurgaon was a different India, an emerging India, and an India very different from the tourist brochures.

Nokia was at its peak in 2006. It opened a new factory to produce mobile phones in India. Unbeknown to all, at that time, Steve Jobs of Apple was developing the iPhone. Apple launched the iPhone in 2007. In a few years after that, they had knocked Nokia off its dominant perch and grabbed the top spot for new mobile phones that were sold. In 2013, Nokia sold its mobile phone business to Microsoft.

It was amazing and in some way a sign of the times that in my own career I had seen the rise and fall of Nokia in such a short time. In some strange way, their rise and fall mirrored my own career. They had risen as I was CEO of Mobitel, my first leadership role. They had sold the business shortly after my final CEO role in Transcend. Nokia still survives, as I do, but in a different role, not at the top but still making a difference, still adding value.

The Nokia sales team had done an excellent job in India. They had won the major market share of building the mobile infrastructure for the mobile operators. The winning streak had started under the leadership of Simon Beresford-Wiley, who moved on from India to lead the APAC region and was at that time in 2005 CEO of Nokia Networks, globally based in Finland. He was followed in India by

Rajiv Suri, who continued the good work done and kept winning more and more contracts. In 2011, Rajiv was appointed the CEO of Nokia, globally.

I knew Simon. He was with Telstra at the same time as me. He had joined as CEO of the Telstra investment in India while I was CEO of Mobitel in Sri Lanka.

The challenge for Nokia in India was now the execution of those contracts the sales team had won. The positon of head of services did not exist. Each account with the customer—such as Airtel, BSNL, Idea, and Vodafone—had their own implementation teams and service teams. My job was to bring the delivery and execution of all of these contracts under one organisation, to build a new team and to drive synergies, to bring in savings, and most importantly, to deliver on time.

It is hard to describe the frenzy, the scale, the emotion, the screaming, the bullying, and the sheer pressure one put on oneself to ride this wave.

We were at our peak, delivering 3,000 new mobile sites every month. A mobile site consists of the 30 M or 40 M steel tower structure, the power required, including diesel generators and batteries, and then the electronics equipment that allows you to have mobile coverage in that area. Each site takes about four months to plan, get all the approvals, and negotiate the land rental with the landlord, then to build. It was a full turnkey contract. The logistics and planning were complicated and involved.

To deliver 3,000 sites to various customers in four months, you had to be planning and developing 4,500 sites in your pipeline. Site acquisition was the major bottleneck. Many landowners did not have documentation to prove they owned the land.

We were building these sites for the customers. They would own the sites. They had to approve the documentation and verify the ownership.

We had about 450 staff in teams all over India, and then more subcontractors helping with the site acquisition and the construction. In the two years, I was in Bangladesh, we had built only 3,000 sites. At that time, that was the largest amount I had built even in a two-year period.

I was now doing this in a month. The 3,000 sites would give you full mobile coverage in Sri Lanka. The sheer scale and the demand from the customer on tight delivery timelines meant this was a very stressful time.

The mobile industry in India was very different and unique in the world. The sheer scale and the ferocity with which the industry grew meant there was no time for technical talent to be nurtured. The only place there was a good resource of radio engineers was the army. The industry grabbed many of the older colonel, majors, and engineers, who all took early retirement and joined the Industry as the technical and engineering team. As a result, the culture was disciplined but also had elements of command and control, had somewhat of a military culture. People knew each other; people knew where they stood with rank.

Just as I was getting used to the role and building a new team, the Vodafone managed-service deal was struck.

This contract meant that Vodafone would transfer 850 of their current staff to us, and we would then fully maintain their mobile network. They were outsourcing their operations and maintenance of the Vodafone network to us. As service head, this would be my responsibility. My role got suddenly more voluminous and complicated. Building new sites was one thing; taking care of a live network and having a 24/7 operation was something else.

Naresh G. was the chief technical officer (CTO) of Vodafone. Together we traversed the country and had town hall meetings with the teams, explained that they were moving from Vodafone to Nokia allow them to ask questions and had all of them sign the letters of transfer. Nokia was a recognised brand, a global brand, as was Vodafone, so there was less concern about the transfer. We embarked on a recruiting spree to recruit the regional leaders as Vodafone had decided to keep back their senior people to monitor our performance and the contract.

I recruited someone from outside the industry, Neetu, as my new executive assistant.

I recently asked her to pen some words about her time working for me that I could include in this book. This would give a different perspective of that time.

> I had the privilege of working with Vijay in early days of my career at Nokia, and some of my learnings with him have enabled me to become a better professional.
>
> Vijay had an eye for detail for everything he did right from formatting PowerPoint slides to spotting the best local shop to eat his favourite Indian snack, viz. *samosas*. He would demand high standards of professionalism from everyone around him. Since I was new to [the] job, I often found myself struggling to ensure that all the relevant content and inputs were available to him to make informed decisions. Vijay would always pre-empt my limitations of being new to [the] job and would ensure that he

made me comfortable by coaching and guiding me for smallest of things. His style was always open and inviting to questions (and expressed appreciation for them), and [he] willingly gave his time to responding to questions thoroughly. Vijay is extremely enthusiastic about his work, which is infectious.

He loved his samosas, and his team members often took this easy, gastronomic path to keep him in gay spirits before/after tough business meetings. Vijay is a family man and loved traveling across the city. An interesting episode, which I can never forget, is of his travel trip to Jaipur where his car was bumped both from front and rear by two different set of stray cattle on the road. I am sure Vijay will never dare to drive to Jaipur alone.

In 2007, Nokia combined its telecom infrastructure business with the infrastructure business of Siemens to form Nokia Siemens Networks or NSN.

The pace of growth, the sheer volumes and scale involved coupled with a very demanding set of customers meant the job as head of services was full on.

I took my responsibility seriously, and it sapped the life out of me.

In a multinational like Nokia, there are countless layers of management, and then you have the matrix structure. It's relatively easy to be in a senior position and avoid taking any responsibility for a missed target or error. It was easy to play the blame game.

If you lead a team, it's important as a leader to stump up and take responsibility even for your team's mistakes.

Leadership ultimately is about taking responsibility. An article I wrote and published in the *LMD* captures this as follows:

> In the Indian subcontinent, the game of cricket is more than a religion. When confronted with a loss, fans can become an uncontrolled mob, and their anger is vented in ugly violence. Sentiments can turn around very quickly when that same team wins. Celebrations go on throughout the night. This fervour and behaviour were evident in the 2011 World Cup matches between Bangladesh, the West Indies and England. Bangladesh lost their match to the West Indies, and the fans, who had become a mob, stoned the West Indies bus leaving the stadium. They had mistakenly thought the bus was carrying the Bangladeshi team. The home of the Bangladesh captain, Shakib Al Hasan, was also stoned. A few days later, the Bangladesh team beat England in Chittagong, and the celebrations blocked all roads and continued through the night.
>
> It's a huge responsibility placed on the young captains aged in their late twenties and early thirties. Yet the current crop of captains are leaders who accept their responsibility, credit the team when they win and "cop it" when they lose.
>
> In Australia, they don't stone the captain's house, but the loss of the Ashes to England in the summer of 2011 was a devastating blow to the Australian cricket fans, who have for the past few years known only dominance in the game of cricket. Despite the incredible record of the captain, Ricky Ponting, including his record of winning three consecutive

World Cups, his record in the Ashes was the only one that mattered. The loss to England in Australia was the first in twenty-four years. Australia suffered three innings defeats in this series for the first time in its history. Calls for his resignation had begun. To his credit, Ricky has copped it fair taking full responsibility for the loss, including his own poor performance with the bat. An essential trait as a leader, there was no shifting of blame anywhere else. Former England Test Captain Geoffrey Boycott commented, "To be blunt, I couldn't see Australia being as bad as they have been in every department. Starting with your selectors, they've made a right mess of everything they have done." In contrast to the younger Ricky Ponting, the Australian selectors have avoided taking responsibility. It was widely reported that the more experienced and older chairman of the selectors, when asked if he should take some blame for the loss in the Ashes said, "I think we've done a very good job as a selection panel, but the reality is we were totally outplayed." In other words, the disaster had nothing to do with selection.

"A chief is a man who assumes responsibility. He says, 'I was beaten.' He does not say, 'My men were beaten.'"—Antoine de Saint-Exupery.

One of the most enduring and widely reported remarks made by Tony Hayward, the CEO of BP during the Deepwater Horizon oil well blowout in the Gulf of Mexico, was, "I want my life back." Asked while touring the sludge-stained beaches by reporters as to how he felt about destroying the livelihood of so many struggling Americans, "We're sorry," he said to reporters. "We're sorry for the massive disruption it caused to their lives." Then sounding annoyed: "And, you know, there's no one who wants this thing over more than I do. I'd like my life back."

The comment was insensitive and not appropriate at the height of the crisis when there was still oil spewing from the uncapped well. However, what made the anger of the community affected by the oil spill even worse was when a few days later Tony was seen sailing with his son in the clears waters off the Isle of Wight. This led to the comment back in the US, mockingly saying, "I think he has his life back."

Tony Hayward received the news of the Deep Horizon blow up almost four hours after the event on a voice mail at 7:24 a.m. London time. He had just returned from his morning jog. BP's top executives gathered in a war room at their London headquarters. It is reported that one of his first comments to his colleagues when they met was, "What the hell did we do to deserve this?" The comment is more significant than the comment he made later about getting his life back. In this comment, his perspective is that BP had done nothing wrong. He blamed everyone else—the contractors, the blowout preventer, everything other than BP.

As leader, his refusal to accept the responsibility led to all of his subsequent PR disasters, and he became a lightning rod for all the anger and hatred of the people affected by the oil spill that went on for eighty-seven days. He ultimately lost his job. He had failed after thirty-five months in the role, in his first real test, to demonstrate his leadership qualities.

Taking responsibility is a fundamental trait of a true leader.

"As human beings, we are endowed with freedom of choice, and we cannot shuffle off our responsibility upon the shoulders of God or nature. We must shoulder it ourselves. It is our responsibility."— Arnold Toynbee

The new NSN had many teething struggles as it tried to integrate the two teams of people globally. The Siemens culture and the Nokia culture were very different. A position as head of services in Asia South, a position in Kuala Lumpur, Malaysia, had opened up, and I was asked if I was interested. The position was to oversee the business in four countries—Malaysia, Philippines, Singapore, and Sri Lanka.

We moved from Gurgaon to Kuala Lumpur. Kuala Lumpur was a much more relaxed city and easier to live in. We were closer to Sydney. It was a big change. In India, you're constantly confronted with the poverty and crowds of people. Working, you are constantly confronted with the sheer scale of everything and competitive nature of everyone. You are faced with bullying and intimidation by the customer who demanded attention and servitude that tore at your dignity.

It was exciting riding the wave, but there was so much you could take of it. I had enjoyed it and was grateful for the opportunity to experience that once-in-a-lifetime wave of explosive growth. It was like a drug, addictive and yet it sapped the very life out of you.

The role in Malaysia was very different to the one I had left in India. The challenge was bringing two very different teams together, to continue the business without interruption, and not have the customers to feel any of the turmoil that was going on with the merger.

It was in Malaysia in 2007 that I discovered the "not-so-silent killer." There was not much information about this affliction, and no one had mentioned this potential killer to me. Later I discovered that, in fact, many members of my family had the affliction and were taking preventative actions.

In India, Sharadha, my wife, had complained about the loud snoring during my sleep. She would be annoyed, but she got used to it; she put up with it. Some nights she would wake me up, as during the night the snoring would suddenly stop, and I was holding my breath. I was holding my breath for so long she had got worried and shook me to get me breathing again. I ignored this condition and did not think much of it.

Over time, the symptom of this affliction was that I was feeling tired in the morning. It was as if I had not had a good night's sleep. In India, coupled with the very stressful role I was having, the condition did not help. I had put down the tiredness in the morning to stress of the job.

In Malaysia, although the job had changed and was not as stressful, the symptoms remained. One morning, driving to work on the highway, I nodded off to sleep. I had a micro sleep. This shook me.

I did some research and found out about obstructive sleep apnea (OSA), the "not-so-silent killer."

OSA is a disorder or affliction characterized by a reduction or pause of airflow (breathing) during sleep. This disruption in my natural breathing pattern triggers the body to violently awaken itself with a rush of adrenaline. Essentially, the cardiovascular system is shocked into awakening me to prevent damage to the body or, more importantly, death.

This disruption in my breathing pattern can happen several times during the night, and episodes can actually stop me from breathing for several minutes. Most people like myself who suffer from sleep apnea do not remember the episodes, but it can result in daytime exhaustion.

The traumatic sleep apnea episodes negatively affect the heart, which is why many individuals who suffer have a higher risk of cardiovascular disease, stroke, high blood pressure, and arrhythmias. Sleep apnea can also cause sleep deprivation, which many believe is a leading cause of auto-related accidents.

The micro sleep while driving was my wake-up call.

I decided to consult a doctor. He recommended a sleep test where I would spend one night in the hospital, and they would rig me up with sensors to monitor my sleep. I had acute obstructive sleep apnea; I was only getting 20 percent of the oxygen my organs needed during my sleep.

The solutions were either a lifetime of sleeping with a CPAP machine or surgery. Surgery, the doctor said, was no guarantee to stop the affliction; if you can put up with it, try the machine.

After some initial trials and errors, I have got a comfortable combination of mask and machine. I don't think about it as an inconvenience or encumbrance. After seven years, it is part of my routine as I prepare for bed. I travel with it everywhere. It has made such a difference to my life.

I had this feeling of being disengaged, a feeling that I was observing my own life, with no control. Once I got used to the machine, I was having deep and quiet sleeps. The machine, an Australian invention, gently pushes air into your nasal passages. It senses your breathing and only increases the pressure ever so slightly when it senses your air passage closing. It is a continuous, positive airway pressure (CPAP) machine. My machine has a humidifier as well to keep the throat from getting dry.

My life, engagement in work, and motivation improved.

In 2008, I was being offered another opportunity to be CEO of a start-up. I was fifty-three years old. I felt good, motivated, but also was acutely aware I was not young anymore, and the younger generation of leaders were coming through. The younger generation of leaders were Asians educated in the United States with MBAs and, with new thinking, were being preferred for the few CEO positions in the region.

The wisdom and experience of doing a start-up, though, could not be learnt at any MBA program.

The Tower Infrastructure business started in the late '90s in the USA. Australia had embraced it, and Crown Castle, a US-based company, was dominant in Australia. The other US company that was a significant player in the industry was American Tower. In Asia, only Indonesia had embraced the model. India was about to do so.

At the start of the mobile communication explosion when the companies were trying to grab customers and expand their coverage into new areas, every mobile operator wanted to build their own infrastructure. It was a competitive edge. As the industry grew, it was becoming unsightly and a waste of funds to duplicate this infrastructure all over the country. It was becoming clear that a sharing model, where an independent tower infrastructure company would build the infrastructure and share it, was more sensible. The mobile operators would pay a monthly lease for the space they took. They would not need to invest in capital expenditure (capex); they would have only an operational expenditure (opex).

This was a real estate business.

In 2008, the Indian government issued 122 new mobile licenses.

I was being offered the opportunity to pioneer the independent tower infrastructure industry in India. I was being offered the position of founding managing director and chief executive officer (CEO) of Transcend Infrastructure based out of Kolkata.

An opportunity to get back on this large wave in India, to bring mobile communications for the first time to some rural areas of the east and northeast of India.

As the new industry was being shaped in India, a few Australian investors, many of who were my colleagues in Telstra, had teamed up with Babcock and Brown, a private-equity investment bank, and started Transcend Infrastructure in Kolkata. Two key executives from Crown Castle in Australia had left that company and were leading the establishment of the new venture. They were based in Singapore.

They had strategized that there was no other independent tower company focussed on East India. It was also the area of least coverage and would be the place mobile operators would want towers built so they could share. Mobile operators were finding that the business case for constructing infrastructure on their own in this poor area of India was not viable. If an independent party such as Transcend could construct and they could share, it was viable.

The challenge in building infrastructure in this area was that this was the equivalent of the "wild west" of India. The area included the states of Bihar, West Bengal, Orissa, and then the seven sister states. The seven sister states were Assam, Arunachal Pradesh, Meghalaya, Manipur, Mizoram, Nagaland, and Tripura. The seven states are connected to the mainland by a slender piece of land called the Silliguri Corridor. This corridor was flanked by Nepal and Bangladesh. The states bordered China, and some of the areas were part of the disputed lands that had resulted in war. Foreigners were prevented from going to the area.

The region was dominated by the Naxalites and the thugs and criminals who had political support. Rape and kidnapping were commonplace. Building communication sites in the rural parts of this territory had its share of risks that had to be managed. Roads and access were poor. There was no electricity in most of this region of India.

I recruited and built a good local team. My wife and I moved to Kolkata from Kuala Lumpur.

Kolkata was more densely populated that Dhaka, but I did not feel it was so crowded. Kolkata had been the capital of British India when they first arrived. The history and culture were very apparent, and the city was vastly different to New Delhi. Poverty was very evident in the streets. Once you see the squalor and the conditions, you get to appreciate what Mother Theresa really did, the compassion she had for the elderly and destitute.

The people were Bengali, and I could see the similarity with the people I had led in Bangladesh.

They were emotional, they were cultured, and they talked a lot. They were keen to learn, and it was a pleasure to lead them.

We had several incidents of our staff being kidnapped and held for ransom in Jharkhand and Assam. In some of the other border states, the local mafia insisted we recruit locals they recommended. In spite of these challenges, we built over 325 towers in East India and the northeast.

I had recruited Moushumi as my PA. I asked her recently to pen a few words on what it was like at Transcend.

It was a pleasure working with you.

You showed so much of exuberance & excitement to start up with Transcend in each and every department & maintained it throughout.

You were very systematic & meticulous about each and everything.

You gave importance to all the team members from senior management team to junior level & hence you started 'Coffee with Vijay' to know your employees better.

You acknowledged good manpower.

You are honest & prudent in dealing with different types of people working under you.

You are very human; at times, people take undue advantage of it.

It was a good learning experience while working
with you & would like to follow whatever you
taught me in my career.

In 2011, the financial crisis that had started in the United States
a few years earlier with the subprime mortgages was spreading.
European ministers agreed to a bailout of Ireland for 85 billion
Euros. Greece had to be rescued for the second time. The bank
Babcock and Brown had gone into liquidation. The funding to keep
the business growing had dried up.

The shareholders decided that the best option was to sell the business
and started looking for potential investors. Depending on the
investor buying the business, my job as CEO was done. I wanted
to return to Sydney. My daughter Naomi was getting married in
November.

In 2011, American Tower acquired the company. I decided to return
to Sydney.

Chapter 10

Leaving a Legacy

Baby boomers are defined as those who were born in the years from 1946 to 1964. It is estimated that in the USA alone there are 75 million people who were born during this period and still living. Having grown up with the music of Elvis, the Beatles, the Rolling Stones, and Woodstock, those born in the early part of the period are now reaching retirement age.

Many born in the first year of the baby boom who had survived would have reached the milestone associated with the Beatles song. They would have been sixty-four in 2010. For most of those born in the 1950s, this is their golden age. Most are now at the peak of their careers; many already having peaked with one career, have changed careers. Some are cruising into early retirement. The majority, though, are happy to keep working, happy to be healthy, working out in a gym, walking or jogging, and eating healthy. Most can expect to live longer than their parents. This generation has lived through and driven the longest period of continuous economic growth in history.

I am a baby boomer. I was born slap bang in the middle of that period, and in 2015, all of us born in 1955 and who have survived will be reaching sixty years of age.

We have no choice about the timing of our birth. But I count it as a blessing that God chose to put me here in 1955. A few million other babies were born in 1955, among them Bill Gates, the person who was the fastest to come from nothing to be the richest man in the world. He transformed our world by giving us the software to increase the speed at which we access and interact with personal computers. Among them, Rowan Atkinson, someone who made more people around the world laugh, transcending language barriers with the character "Mr. Bean." Just to grow in this period and see the transformation of the world from the time of no computers to the wonder that was the Internet, e-mail, Skype; the growth of television from black and white to colour and all those other wonderful tools that brought us, as a world closer, was such a blessing, I could not think of a better time to be on earth and to be sixty.

It was while reflecting on my life for this book that I came to understand how we are faced with many choices in life. Some choices challenge our status quo or comfort zone more than others. These choices are doors, doors that we choose to open or not. There is no right choice or wrong choice. If we open the door, there are risks, but also an opportunity to grow, an opportunity to find the purpose of our lives. If we never open the door, we will still be comfortable in the life we lead but may miss an opportunity to find out the man or woman we could be.

Every door we open has its risks; every door we open has its rewards. Some doors may be locked from the inside after a short time, meaning that some choices have a limited window of opportunity. Procrastinating and taking time to make a choice may close that particular door forever. Doing nothing and being comfortable with the status quo is also a choice. But it also has its risks. The ground can shift. The environment and circumstances can change. The comfortable status quo can change. When this happens, instead of a choice, we will have an ultimatum. We are forced to make a decision. There is no longer a choice.

The best advice I have read in making a choice is to assume failing is impossible. This allows us to make bolder choices. Ultimately, I believe, it really does not matter about the outcome or result, whatever choice we make. It is really about the experience and change. Change allows us to grow. Unless we grow, we will not progress in life. We will be stagnant. We will never be the person we ought to be.

I believe that there is no such thing as fate. We have immense power in determining the choices we make. I read somewhere that "fate always gives you two choices—the one you should have taken and the one you do."

We have the liberty to choose; God has given us that right. Whether we pray before making the choice—as I have done so many times—or not, it's still our choice. Yet if the other option turned out to be better, we nearly always tend to blame it on fate. There is, however, no wrong and right. Every choice gives us the opportunity to learn and grow. It's by making mistakes that we learn and grow the most.

For me, to be involved in the explosive growth of the telecommunications industry that helped people get closer and to give them the tools to lift many of them out of poverty was a blessing. To bring mobile communications for the first time to many rural parts of Sri Lanka, Bangladesh, and the northeast of India would have been enough. I know the difference that made to many families. To be part of the explosive growth of mobile phones in India, growing from zero to 400 million in a space of fourteen years, was amazing. I was witness to the transformation that this technology, this communication tool, made to the one billion people of that country; the change was palpable. It was a blessing to be born in this time and to ride that wave.

We are, though, constantly reminded of our mortality; this is but a short interlude in the journey of our soul.

It was a bright and cool winter day in Delhi in February 2007. I was country director of services for Nokia in India and was based in Gurgaon, close to Delhi. I was leading a team of over 1,500 staff, our own and contractors. We were breaking all records in the delivery to our customers of mobile communication sites. Building these sites with large towers was a complex civil and mechanical engineering task.

Just before going to work that morning, my father had spoken to me and mentioned that my mother was admitted to hospital. He did not betray any urgency in his conversation, and yet I detected a strain and stress I had not heard from him before. I decided that I would plan to visit them in the coming days. I asked him if he needed me there immediately, and he said he could manage. I was on my way to work, when I got a call from my wife Sharadha. Her mother had told her that things were more critical than we had gathered from the call earlier that morning. I immediately booked flights; Sharadha and I flew that evening down to Colombo in Sri Lanka.

My mother was seventy-five; she had just recovered from the flu and had a residual chest infection. On that day, she had difficulty breathing, and my father had driven her to the emergency room at the hospital. Her condition was worse than first thought, and she was gasping for air. The heart was deprived of oxygen, and just as she got to the hospital, she stopped breathing; her heart stopped. If not for the timely arrival at the emergency unit of Durdans hospital in Colombo and the intervention of a young doctor there who took immediate responsibility and revived her, she would be dead.

It was a stressful few days as we watched her struggle to cling to life, harder for a son to see his mother so helpless, with numerous tubes and needles keeping her breathing and alive. She fought like a warrior, she fought to stay alive, and you could sense the fight every time you went into the ICU and stood by her bed. She was not about to give up. When I asked her later what she experienced at the emergency unit as she was brought in, she said she had very little recall of anything, but she remembers a journey down a tunnel and a name board with the word *death* passing by.

Over the next few weeks, she recovered, luckily without any permanent damage either to her heart or brain. Over the year, her health improved, and she regained her strength. She had a goal, to get fit enough to travel in August 2008 to see her eldest grandson, Prashanth, get married in Toronto, Canada. Her world revolves around the family and my father. The family was just about to celebrate and get larger, with her grandchild getting married, and it was not the time to go. One can only speculate on the struggle she went through during those critical days; she would have had a choice to give up, to succumb to the peace of death. She chose to continue with the celebration of her life. Her legacy was her children, her grandchildren, and they were reaching a special time in their life. She wanted to be there. My mother was reminded of her mortality, and the experience changed her in many ways. She chooses now to take every day as a blessing, to live everyday as a celebration of her life.

Recently, a very good friend who now lives in England had gone in for a routine blood test. The results seemed normal, and the GP gave him a clean bill of health. His daughter, though, who had recently passed out as a doctor, read the results and noticed something amiss. After further consultations, it was discovered that he had a rare terminal disease. The daughter happened to be working in a hospital at that time that had the leading specialist of that particular rare disease. The result, after many more tests and consultations with the specialist, was that he had disease of the blood that was life threatening, but the early detection would give him a bit longer than most of those with this particular disease. Most who are afflicted tend to detect it very much later as there are no visible symptoms. We have no choice in our ending as we had no choice of our beginning. But we have a choice to continue to seek the purpose of our lives, to challenge the status quo, and each bit of news, such as that which was given to my friend, opens the door to reassess and invigorate the quest for seeking this purpose.

I admire Bill Gates for a number of reasons but most of all for his choice to have a second career, to reinvent himself, to learn about diseases and medicine, and to use his fortune built on computers to eradicate several viruses that were not of the computing kind but those that were threatening children in Africa and Asia. He created the world's largest charitable organisation with his wife and with his dad as co-chair, working to distribute a staggering $27.5 billion in a number of countries. Here was a man, the richest in the world, who had a comfortable life, had worked hard to get to be chairman of Microsoft. He could continue to live and enjoy the fruits of his labour. If anyone could claim to have found his purpose in life, it was him. He had transformed the world. He had a choice, though, to not to be content, to challenge the status quo, to investigate if the purpose of his life was something else. He, with a lot of guidance from his wife, Melinda, chose to reinvent himself, to undertake another mission to change the world in a different way. This was more spiritual than about self. He had done enough to leave a lasting legacy as the co-founder of Microsoft, the company that changed the world. Yet he may be remembered for something far greater if he achieves his mission of eradicating the world of certain diseases.

Then there is Nandan Nilekani, also born in 1955, completed a career as the co-founder of Infosys, a company that changed India, gave birth to the whole IT-outsourcing industry, and he made a fortune in the process. Yet like Bill Gates, not satisfied to enjoy the fruits of his success, cruising with the billions he made, maintaining the status quo, he chose to take another path. He wanted to create the defining database of all Indians, a tool that would deliver help to all Indians in need at the right time and in their village—a mammoth undertaking in any country but here the challenge was that India was a country of over a billion people. He resigned his post as head of Infosys and joined the government to spearhead the project. Success here would mean a legacy left for a billion people.

What about us? What is it that we leave behind when we leave this world? How will we want to be remembered? Will we really care, considering that we will be in a better place with, I presume, new challenges? Wherever we are, I believe we will have no memory of this life. It will be like wiping the hard disk clean—no memory of that wonderful holiday, no memory of a wife or your children, just a blank.

Those left behind, though, will have memories of you. All of us will certainly leave behind memories. Our close family and friends will fondly remember those special moments they shared with us—each interaction, each special smile, the way we laughed and cried, and the food we liked—but these memories will also fade with time. Is that why we live? Just to leave some memories behind.

Charles Handy writes about the components of a good life as living, learning, loving, and leaving a legacy. He uses the psychologist Abe Maslow's theory on the hierarchy of needs to describe life as a ladder. The first rung is survival. Once we leave home, can we survive on our own, get a qualification, earn a living, and raise a family? Once survival is in no doubt, we then need to express ourselves, stand out from the crowd, establish some unique identity, maybe live in the better suburbs, and buy a bigger house. For most of us, success in midlife is reaching this rung of the ladder.

He goes on to write, "But the ladder does not stop there. We still yearn to leave our mark on the world, to make an imprint and leave it a little different because we lived for good or ill. The last rung on that ladder, therefore, is that of 'contribution' to something bigger than ourselves, our private bid for immortality, for some lasting memorial."

It is only natural to want to be somebody. We want to be well thought of, and we want to achieve a result. If I am not wise, I want to become wise. If I am a person that tends to get angry, I want to be less angry. The becoming is a choice.

The ambition to become the best musician or the perfect saint is a conscious series of choices. The choice made to make sacrifices, to struggle, to practice, practice and practice. In his book, *Talent Is Overrated,* Geoff Colvin states that the conventional wisdom about "the natural" is a myth. He introduces the concept of deliberate practice. Deliberate practice requires that one identify certain sharply defined elements of performance that need to be improved, and then work intently on them. Tiger Woods, for example, has been seen to drop golf balls into a sand trap and step on them, and then practice shots from that near impossible lie. The real path to great performance is a matter of choice. So the bottom line is that all of us have it in us to be a Tiger Woods or a Bill Gates. To leave that kind of a lasting legacy, it's a choice—to be known as the greatest golfer of all time, to be remembered as the co-founder of Microsoft. The question is: How bad do you want it? Most of us are happy going with the flow, the deliberate practice required to be a Tiger Woods is too cumbersome to contemplate. It's just great to admire his choice, appreciate the deliberate practice and work he has put in to acquire the skill that helps him beat others in the game.

Every one of us, however, will leave a legacy. Just being a father of Bill Gates is the legacy of Bill Gates Snr. Earl Woods had a pivotal part in the grooming, nurturing, and persevering with the deliberate practice to enable the success of Tiger Woods. In an article in *Fortune* magazine on the "Best Advice I Ever Got," Tiger Woods recalls: "When I was young, maybe six or seven years old, I'd play on the navy golf course with my pop. My dad would say, 'Okay, where do you want to hit the ball?' I'd pick a spot and say, 'I want to hit it there.' He'd shrug and say, 'Fine, then figure out how to do it.' He didn't position my arm, adjust my feet, or change my thinking. He just said go ahead and hit that darn ball. My dad's advice to me was to simplify. He knew that at my age I couldn't digest all of golf's intricacies. He kept it simple."

All fathers and mothers, if anything, leave the legacy of their children and have some part contributed to the achievements of the generations beyond.

I don't seek a legacy; it is what it is. It is enough to be the husband of Sharadha and be witness to her selfless giving. It is enough to be the father of our children, Viruben and Naomi. I am a witness to their growth and their career advancement, one as a naval officer and avionics engineer and the other as a successful marketer. I am also acutely aware of the number of young people I have touched and given a hand up, picked them from obscurity, given them some inspiration to better themselves. They are grateful and have the kept in touch. I consider them too my legacy. I continue, though, to pursue the answer to this question: "What is the purpose of my life?"

I may not find the answer to the question. It is the pursuit of the answer that will make me take some risk, to open doors I might not have opened. In the end, I may not find the answer; it does not matter. The journey in seeking this answer is what matters in the end. It is enough, if they say of me:

"He did the best he could with what he had."

Printed in the United States
by Baker & Taylor Publisher Services